I TRUSTED THE PROCESS

I TRUSTED THE PROCESS

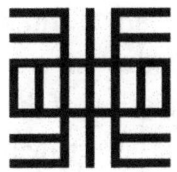

Works from My Sojourn through Seminary

Nicholas A. Meade

Foreword by David A. Jones

Title: I Trusted the Process: Works from My Sojourn through Seminary

Copyright © 2020 Nicholas A. Meade Ministries

Cover Art By:
Keita Johnson

All rights reserved. No part of this publication may be reproduced, distributed, or transmitted in any form or by any means, including photocopying, recording, or other electronic or mechanical methods, without the prior written permission of the publisher, except in the case of brief quotations embodied in critical reviews and certain other noncommercial uses permitted by copyright law.

For permission requests, send an email to the publisher with the subject line "Copyright Permissions" to the following email address:
    Nicholas A. Meade Ministries
    publishing@nicholasmeade.com
    www.nicholasmeade.com

Library of Congress Control Number: 2020905342

ISBN 978-0-9861654-4-3

Contents

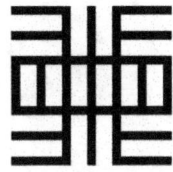

Foreword	vi
Preface	viii
Acknowledgements	xi
Dedication	xiii
Introduction	1
1: Textual	5
2: Historical	39
3: Practical	91
4: Theological	128
5: Reflective	172
Bibliography	201

Foreword

I Trusted the Process. What a fitting title for a work that conveys the mature and still-multiplying fruit of one who moved by faith through a process that forever altered the trajectory of his life. I, along with all of the countless others who matriculated at the Samuel DeWitt Proctor School of Theology, have experienced that same sense of having our theological umbilical cords severed that we might discover new life beyond the womb of an uncritical fundamentalism.

I first encountered Nicholas Meade as a budding scholar, a few years my junior, who already possessed a keen intellect, an analytical mind, and an openness to new ideas. It was his commitment to excellence; however, that grabbed my attention. As an engineer, he already knew how systems could be built, redesigned, and integrated with other systems both old and new. All of this was in service of furthering the performance capabilities of those systems.

Nick applied this same acumen to the theological task. He was able to integrate and synthesize new information and perspectives and incorporate them into his own inchoate understanding of the academic disciplines. A product of a theologically and doctrinally conservative tradition, he was not a prisoner of that tradition. He did not dismiss facts, whether historical or textual, in order to preserve any religious or ecclesiastical anachronisms. In other words, he respected the traditions that had been bequeathed to him, but he was unafraid to challenge, modify, or discard them when they could not stand under the light of truth or when they threatened to impede the progress of God's people.

In this respect, I think we discern Dr. Meade's real value for the 21st century church. His journey mirrors, and I believe will help advance, the journey of the Black Church. We as a people were bequeathed a religion that had become distorted through racial and cultural accretions to serve our oppression. But we, as a people, trusted the process. As we would come to sing:

> *Stony the road we trod, bitter the chastening rod,*
> *Felt in the days when hope unborn had died;*
> *Yet with a steady beat, have not our weary feet*
> *Come to the place for which our people sighed?"*

Dr. Nicholas Meade stood out among the very gifted Class of 2012 as a man who honored the past not as a prison to be forever bound in, but as a departure point for spiritual, intellectual, theological, political, and physical liberation. Nicholas Meade has come to a place of understanding about God, scripture, and community for which our ancestors but sighed. The road was stony, filled with the chastening rod of homiletical critiques, theological deconstruction and reconstruction, and the hope of an academic degree yet unborn. Nick trusted the process, and moved with a steady beat, driven by the rhythmic pounding of the drums of the ancestors in his spirit.

I heartily commend this spiritual and theological memoir to an audience that I know will draw both inspiration and encouragement from the shared experiences of a fresh new voice in religious studies. I have personally enjoyed revisiting this golden chapter of our lives: the anxiety before preaching, the impending deadlines of exegetical papers, the intriguing after-class discussions, and those damnable group projects! I thank my friend Nick for his courage in sharing his journey. I enjoin those who peruse these pages to, as you read, remember to trust the process!

Rev. Dr. David A. Jones
Pastor of Williams Memorial Baptist Church
Seminary Classmate

Preface

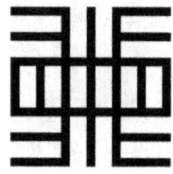

I Trusted the Process came into being as the result of my faith journey through seminary in pursuit of my Master of Divinity degree at the Samuel DeWitt Proctor School of Theology at Virginia Union University in Richmond, Virginia. Part of the inspiration for compiling selected works from my sojourn through seminary into this work derives from my interaction with some of the previous seminary work from Dr. Martin Luther King, Jr. Fortunately, pieces of his work from those formative years still exist and is available to be studied by current seminarians. I consider myself privileged for the opportunity to wrestle with his thinking while I wrestled with my own.

At the same time, I chose to publish this book as a means of further contributing to my legacy by compiling works from that critical time in my theological development in order to provide a sample of work and a snapshot of my thoughts in process. The beneficiaries of this look back in time include not simply seminarians enduring their own process of wrestling with their theology, but also those who maintain interest in the process undertaken by those who serve them in ministry. Selfishly, perhaps, I also desired to leave a glimpse of my mind to my children and future generations who could prayerfully read their ancestor's words with pride and gratitude. After my first weekend in seminary, I knew that the experience would be transformative and life changing. By compiling this work, I have provided more understanding as to the making of a theologian.

The cover images have special meaning. The ankh, the original cross, reflects my seminary education's ties to Africa as it represents eternal and physical life. As a black man, this is special because it reminds me of Christianity's ties to North Africa. The open book images reflect the search for knowledge and the illumination found in seminary. The stacked rocks reflect the holistic nature of seminary education and how it affects each of the stones. Mother Emanuel AME Church in Charleston, South Carolina, the site where African American worshippers were killed due to hate reflects seminary's empowerment to fight for liberation and how faith made our people more resilient. The worshiping people reflects the seminary's connection to worship; both learning about proper worship and participating in worship through chapel. Lastly, the Adinkra symbol in the middle with African colors, "Nea Onnim No Sua A, Ohu," means "one who does not know can know from learning." This symbol was on my stole as I graduated with my Master of Divinity. The pursuit it symbolizes never truly ends.

How does the process of seminary transform? Why do you believe what you believe? What are some effective methods for preaching? How can one be empowered to minister to the masses? *I Trusted the Process* is a reflection upon how one's sojourn through seminary answers these questions. Join me on a journey back in time where my experience or process in seminary transformed me and profoundly shifted the way that I think and minister. While some cast doubt on the worth of seminary, even going to the great lengths of labeling it a cemetery, my works collected in this volume from my time in seminary show how seminary can challenge someone; challenging that someone to the extent that if that someone trusts the process, that someone will come out better on the other side.

I Trusted the Process provides models and example work from seminary that readers can use to do their own work of determining what they believe and why. Works within this volume also provide examples of biblical exegesis, preaching methodologies at work, reflections on written works and of holistic ministry, and a pattern for articulating one's own Christology, among other things. Navigating through this book for those unable to attend seminary can serve as its own type of process. It also provides insight into the mind of one who seeks to help change the world. If one is to believe the glowing words from the foreword and the cover, such a mind is worth exploration. *I Trusted the Process*. Can you?

My prayer is that this work not only blesses my future generations and seminarians, but all who read this as they wrestle with their own theologies. As God revealed Godself to me during my time of development, I believe that God is still revealing Godself through seminary and other means. May the words of my mouth and the mediations of my heart serve as a catalyst for the theological development of all who hear and read them.

Acknowledgements

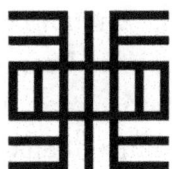

One of my favorite quotes from my all-time favorite television show is from the show *A Different World*. At a banquet that honored the contributions and legacy of the character named Colonel Bradford Taylor, the honoree, during his acceptance speech said something that I will never forget. He said: "A man can go to the top of a hill and plant a flag; but no man can make it to the top of that hill alone." These words ring true of my sojourn through seminary; and therefore, this space serves as a place from which I can express my gratitude.

To the Godhead, I give all honor, glory, and praise for the three years I spent being shaped by some of the greatest minds in the church and Christian scholarship. To that end, I must acknowledge all of my professors, and in particular Dr. Adam Bond, for the challenge and for the excellence with which they approached their ministry of the academy. I also want to acknowledge my Dean, Dr. John Kinney, for all of the wonderful words of encouragement and theological insight over the years. Every instructor made her or his mark; and I am grateful for all of them.

I must also thank God for my classmates with whom I completed many group projects over the years. During my time in seminary, I developed friends for life and these bonds were formed through debate, fellowship and friendship. We trusted the process and made it through together. The number of friends I would like to mention in this space is many so I will concisely state that I thank God for all of you.

Lastly, but of course, not least I express gratitude for my family. Tanesha Meade you mean the world to me and this journey would have been impossible without your understanding and support. To the two children I had when I finished – Brenton & Brielle – thank you! To my other two children that we had after I earned the degree and who along with their older siblings benefit from having a dad with a clearer theology – Braeyen & Brooklan – thank you! To all the relatives, in particular my parents and in-laws who stepped in when my wife needed your assistance because I was traveling for school, I express my gratitude.

I was able to finish my sojourn through seminary only with you all.

Dedication

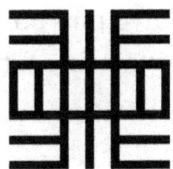

This work is dedicated to every professor, classmate, seminarian, and every other person engaged with interrogating and studying your faith and beliefs. God can handle your questions.

For surely I know the plans I have for you, says the Lord, plans for your welfare and not for harm, to give you a future with hope.
– Jeremiah 29:11 NRSV

Introduction

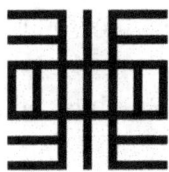

"My name is Nicholas Meade and I was born in Baltimore, Maryland and raised in the city of Severn. My mother started taking my brother and me since I was around ten years old to her home church – Silas First Baptist Church of Severna Park. It wasn't long after being in church consistently that I accepted Jesus Christ as my Lord and Savior and was baptized. After that I became heavily involved in church activities beginning with the youth choir and the usher board. The salvation of my father led me to attend additional church services and through the years of fellowship and studying I absorbed more of God's Word.

Eventually in 1998 I graduated from high school in the top three percent of my class and went on to study at the University of Maryland at College Park. Along with other top incoming freshmen I was invited to participate in the university's Honors and Gemstone Programs. I accepted both invitations and eventually earned citations for completing both programs. During my college years I was also involved in the school chapter of the Black Engineers Society and once was honored as Member of the Year. After much hard work, in May 2003, the university awarded me a B.S. degree in computer engineering.

In 1999 after growing stronger in the faith I sensed that something was still missing and sought the Lord's will for my life. Through His Word and prayer He revealed that I would preach and teach His Word and this surprised me even though God had begun to expose my gifts. Just before graduating with my degree I felt God's call on my life to the preaching ministry and after much prayer and fasting I answered the call of God to proclaim His Word. After sharing the news with my pastor, I was given the opportunity to preach my initial sermon on July 6, 2003 and became a licensed associate minister. Over the years I have had numerous responsibilities within my church including Youth and Young Adult Ministry Co-leader, Sunday School, Youth Bible Study, and Vacation Bible School instructor. My goal has been to glorify God in all that I do because I take my calling and the responsibility of ministry very seriously.

I anticipate using this theological education to supplement my gifts and to be further prepared for a life of ministry. Another goal is to use the skills and methods learned at the School of Theology to grow in the work of preaching and teaching. My studies will also cause me to dig even deeper into God's word so that I can be an effective minister during such times as these. It is my desire to earn a Masters of Divinity degree that includes field education so that I can better apply theology and ministry and to also "learn through the provision of service and the practice of ministry" as the catalog says and open my mind to the possibilities of ministry."

The above words comprised the element of my application for seminary known as my personal statement. In it, I articulated why seminary and why then. Looking back, I clearly underestimated the affect that seminary would have on me as a preacher, teacher, theologian, as well as the affect it would have on me as a believer in the Christian faith. Prior to seminary, I viewed most things in terms of black and white without any shades of gray. Oftentimes, I tell others of how I began seminary as a fundamentalist but graduated liberated of many of the poor theologies and biases that led me to arrogantly categorize and minimize the contributions or theologies or spiritualties of others. Graduation for me marked my emancipation from such things and my work during those transformative years reflects this.

Introduction

Some elements of my seminary experience are not completely captured in the pages that follow due to their experiential nature. In other words, there are experiential elements of seminary that had an impact although my thought process through those elements is difficult because they required no assignments that shed light on my psyche. However, I must reflect upon them because they are critical elements that help to make seminary worthwhile. One of such experiences is the experience of Saturday chapel where a choir composed of students and faculty took turns preaching an encouraging message. Worship was always rich, and we always seemed to leave chapel feeling better and prepared to tackle class for the day. Dean Kinney always provided the cherry on top as he would often offer remarks that would send students scrambling for paper and pen in order to jot down shared nuggets. Chapel is one of the reasons why there is no place like seminary and is one of the reasons that I miss seminary to this day.

Other elements of ministry included a yearlong course entitled "Formation for Ministry." Part of that course included a psychological assessment in the form of the Myers Briggs assessment. Through that assessment I was able to ascertain a label for my unique personality. My assessment resulted in a profile type of "ISTJ," an abbreviation for introversion, sensing, thinking, and judging. In one of the handouts we received, this characterized me as the "most responsible" who is "doing what should be done." Further, I was characterized as organized, compulsive, private, trustworthy, practical and one who follows rules and regulations. We also filled out the Holland Interest Code Summary and BarOn Emotional Quotient Inventory in which my results indicated that I was not a fit for ministry since I did not meet the minimum Total EQ of 110. We also took the Strong Interest Inventory and had a Leadership Report from the use of the FIRO-B and MBTI instruments. These courses also reinforced the notion that there are more contexts for ministry other than the church to include the academy and centers for pastoral care.

In the pages that follow, I provide samples of my academic work through my seminary years as I trusted the process. Beginning with our orientation and throughout our time at our beloved STVU, many persons encouraged my classmates and I to trust the process. Faculty and upperclassmen told us to expect deconstruction during our first year, followed by reconstruction during our second year. In other words, our theologies and many of the beliefs we held dear prior to seminary would be demolished or torn down in order to clear room in our hearts for a newly informed theology as we wrestled with clearer understandings of the biblical text and history among other things. While it will be painful, they said, it was necessary, and we should trust the process.

    I trusted the process. Seminary went through me as I went through seminary and my life has never been the same. The chapters that follow show this evolution in thought as it begins with works that fall into a textual category. This first chapter presents my first full exegesis from seminary along with my sermons from each of the three years. The following chapters contain works belonging to historical, practical, theological and reflective categories.

1

Textual

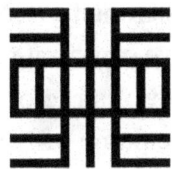

Biblical Studies

Biblical studies or education that empowers persons to wrestle faithfully with the biblical text lies at the heart of seminary education. This is particularly why at STVU the curriculum calls for students to take these foundational courses of Introduction to Biblical Studies, Old Testament and New Testament. Other students informed those of us who took orientation during the fall term of 2009 at STVU that the first year would be the hardest as the seminary took steps to tear down what we believed we knew. This was to properly prepare us so that seminary could rebuild our theology properly using church history and systematic theology during our 'Middler' year. These students were prophetic in that they spoke the truth and they also predicted our futures. The first year where instructors empowered us to rightly divide the word of truth proved to be more challenging than I anticipated. Then again, I expected nothing less than eye-opening instruction. This is because my wife's enrollment in the Bachelor of Nursing program at Notre Dame of Maryland University required her to take courses in religion, and in one of these courses her instructors introduced her to the subject of myths particularly in the Old Testament. My wife proceeded to come home and attempt to explain to her, then fundamentalist husband, that much that he believed with regard to the creation stories of Genesis rested on taking literally myths meant by Moses to explain how the people of Israel came to reside in Egypt before their deliverance.

Eager for more, I applied and enrolled with her support and started my journey attempting to trust the process. Academically, I never lacked confidence in my God-given abilities, but my first term in seminary provided the wakeup call that I needed. Along with an introductory course on the church and its ministry, formation for ministry, and a yearlong field education course, my first term included an introductory course to Biblical Studies. My instructor was a two-time earner of a Ph.D. in Old Testament by the name of Naomi P. Franklin. We learned a great deal in her class, and she exuded the love that she held for the biblical text. This class primarily focused on how to perform a biblical exegesis as opposed to eisegesis. We learned about context and the various forms of criticism, a la historical and redaction criticism, which must inform any sound exegesis.

This class was interesting for several reasons as it relates to our professor, fellow classmates, and it being the first semester in seminary. Dr. Franklin shared stories of her own perseverance related to being an African American woman who broke down barriers in her pursuit of academic excellence. She provided insight into her private life, and due to her background, she held a fondness particularly for Jewish people. Perhaps as a result, one of the tidbits she shared that caused some contention was her interpretation of John 14:6. Believing that there is hope for Jewish brothers and sisters, she stated emphatically that while Jesus is the way, the text never says that Jesus is the only way. On this and other occasions, she clashed with students as they fought to hold on to traditional interpretations of scripture. Many such discussions led to tears on both sides. Her class demonstrated one of the principle jewels of seminary: it provides a safe space and platform in which one's traditional views can find challenge and a space in which one can wrestle with why they believe what they believe. This class was not simply theoretical in nature, but Dr. Franklin's class was invaluable because it required that we execute an exegesis properly.

A biblical exegesis on our own selected passage of scripture became the biggest and most important assignment of the term and the largest contributor to our grade due to unforeseen circumstances. In the end, the B- I earned on the exegesis also became my course grade and the only non-A grade that I received in seminary. This is not stated for the purpose of bragging but reflects the overall process where humbling experiences in which one is broken down sometime precedes others of an edifying nature. Presented below is my exegesis on Jesus and the ten lepers.

Exegesis - Luke 5:12-16 (NRSV)

This narrative from the gospel of Luke is a microcosm of the ministry of Jesus. In this text, Jesus follows His familiar pattern in healing stories and shows Jesus' inclination to break down barriers; Jesus' tendency to effectively minister to the outcasts of society who were in need; Jesus' ability to adjust as circumstances dictated a change; and Jesus' ability to maintain His relationship with the Father through all of this turmoil.

Contextual Analysis

Evidence suggests that the author of the Gospel of Luke was a close friend and traveling companion of Paul named Luke.[1] There exists no uniform belief as to the date of composition but one source suggests that it was written between 61 and 63 AD[2] while another suggests a time between 80 and 100 C.E.[3] There is no agreement from scholars on the place of composition although some believe it to have been composed in Rome[4] or Syrian Antioch.[5] According to the preliminary verses of the Gospel itself it was written to remind Theophilus, who must have some authority, of what he had been taught and it chronicles events that took place in the early part of the first century. Evidence suggests that the author also wanted this Gospel available for a wider readership.[6] Some scholars believe the Two Source Hypothesis[7] while others believe the Griesbach Hypothesis[8] with regard to the sources used to write this gospel. This text falls in the section of Luke that could be called "Jesus' ministry in Galilee" (4:14 – 9:50).[9] "Leprosy in Luke's world is generally not the Hansen's disease of modern times…it was a socioreligious disease" and lepers "were regarded as impure and marginal to normal society."[10] Lepers "were isolated from concourse with the holy people of God in cities" so anyone touching something unclean became unclean and this fact is critical for this pericope.[11] This particular miracle in the text comes in a chapter replete of other miracles including the great catch of fish (vv 1-9) and the healing of the paralytic man (vv 18-25). Jesus also taught the people (vv 1, 17, 21-24, 29-39).

Formal Analysis

The text takes place in the book of Luke which is a Gospel. Chapter 5 of Luke records a collage of different historical events and this selection of text also describes a historical event as evidenced by the author's use of the word "once" at the beginning of the text. This healing story moves "from illness to wholeness" to instruction to increased fame and finally withdrawal.[12] This text is also prose and could be divided into six divisions:
   a) Introduction to people involved (verse 12a)
   b) What the leper does (verse 12b)
   c) What Jesus does (verse 13)
   d) Instructions for the newly clean (verse 14)
   e) Newly clean disregards instructions (verse 15)
   f) Jesus is forced to withdraw (verse 16)

Detailed Analysis

Introduction to people involved (verse 12a)

The leper approaches Jesus in a city, likely Galilee based on the Mark's Gospel account. This "raises the problem of what the afflicted person was doing in a city" and suggests that this leper is willing to break boundaries with the hope that the "ultimate boundary-breaker" could help him.[13] By this time, the lepers would have been likely expelled from the city.[14] Leprosy in the Biblical text is used as a general term that covers several skin diseases and sometimes it resulted in skin discoloration, scaling or itching.[15] If the priest determined that the disease in fact was leprous then the priest would declare the person ceremonially unclean. Lepers were required to wear torn clothing, cover their mouths, and yell "Unclean" when around others but the good news is that leprosy was curable.[16] The physical and social plight of the leper leads the reader to be sympathetic toward the leper.

What the leper does (verse 12b)

The leper comes and bows to Jesus and according to New Testament culture the leper made obeisance to him which was a sign of the leper's belief in the divinity or deity of Christ.[17] The leper begged or desperately pleaded and asked for cleansing. The leper dared Jesus to heal him[18] and in doing so the leper inferred that Jesus had the power to heal him but questioned Jesus' will or desire to do so. By asking to be clean, essentially the leper is asking to be healed of his leprosy so that he can be cleansed by ritual (Leviticus 14:2-4). This was normal for lepers who as a result of their condition were provoked to anguish and desperate supplications.[19]

What Jesus does (verse 13)

The description of this occurrence in Mark 1:40-45 says that Jesus is moved with pity and other ancient sources say He is moved with anger. It could have been anger at the man for disrespecting the law by crashing the barriers."[20] As He often did, Jesus changed how people viewed the law by touching this leper and diffusing the notion that touching a leper made one unclean.[21] To Jesus being unclean had nothing to do with the exterior of a person but "rather that which proceeds from the heart."[22] Using redaction criticism and the Two Source Hypothesis, Luke's account highlights the will and power of Christ in omitting Mark's references to mercy or anger.[23] The man was healed immediately and was able to rejoin the community.[24]

Instructions for the newly clean (verse 14)

Jesus told the man to tell no one but since the man is already healed by the time of this command, Jesus' instructions likely either served as a witness against the priest and costly offerings or a "facetious remark."[25] Jesus told the man to go and show himself to the priest and give an offering. Jesus shows His familiarity and understanding of the Old Testament law. Jesus is referring to the elaborate ritual a former leper had to endure and also referring to the necessity of giving an offering meaning that this was a costly process especially for a leper.

Newly clean disregards instructions (verse 15)

The fame of Jesus spread abroad and people came and gathered to hear Jesus teach and to be healed of their diseases at least partly because the former leper's disregard for Jesus' instructions. The former leper, according the account in Mark 1:40-45, freely proclaims what Jesus had done for him but Luke omits any notion of the former leper's disobedience.

Jesus is forced to withdraw (verse 16)

Jesus had to withdraw to pray and does so in part because His fame prevented Him from being able to enter into a town openly.[26] Jesus praying shows that He maintained His relationship with God in spite of the attack that was coming that begins in with the rest of this chapter.[27]

Synthesis

Throughout this text Jesus breaks down the social and ritualistic barriers to ministry and ministers to a leper who has been outcast from society. Jesus does effectively by not letting the leper leave His presence without the leper being healed. Even after His fame prevented Him from ministering in the city Jesus was able to adjust and withdrew to the country. There Jesus did not grow discouraged but prayed to the Father and demonstrated the resilient relationship that He had with the Father in spite of all that would happen because of His ministry.

Reflection

As it was in the day of Jesus, today there great need in this world. In today's society, the ones who cannot defend themselves and the ones that go without basic necessities are the same ones that are treated as outcasts. The text speaks volumes about God's compassion that needs to be extended through the church of Christ. In other words, just as Jesus cared about the condition of this leper, the church ought to be concerned about the plights of others. Jesus commanded that his disciples should minister to lepers, the outcasts of society (Matthew 10:8), and so as an extension of the ministry of Christ, the church should be ministering to those who are cast down or cast away by society. This means that the church should not be so focused on spiritual things that they neglect the pressing natural needs of others and the positions of these persons in today's society. Dr. Martin Luther King Jr. once said "Any religion which professes to be concerned about the souls of men and is not concerned about the social and economic conditions that scar the soul, is a spiritually moribund religion only waiting for the day to be buried."[28] The surest way for the gospel to become dead to the world is for the church to neglect its ministry to the outcasts of society.

Old Testament

The second floor of Ellison Hall served as the class location for the Introduction to Biblical Studies and the Introduction to Old Testament courses. The lecturer was an ABD student by the name of Sandy Rogers. She provided fresh insight into the world of the Old Testament and challenged many of our prior held beliefs. As it was in the previous course, students struggled with some of the things she shared including how the creation stories were a collection of myth, not in the sense of fables, but stories told and handed from one generation to another in an attempt to provide reasons for the origins of their reality. She taught us about the propagandist aims of the Deuteronomic

Historian and how many of the claims made in the historical books do not align with extrabiblical support.

Rogers shared interesting tidbits that reinforced the notion of context, and how interpretation absent of context is flawed. She demonstrated this by discussing, for example, how "feet" in the Old Testament was a euphemism for male genitalia as seen in the story of Boaz and Ruth, and David attempting to coverup his sin by getting Uriah to "wash his feet" or have intercourse with his wife. I am grateful for her investment in us. One interesting thing about her class is that she gave us the option of writing a paper or taking exams for our midterm and final exams. Each time, I was one of two persons who opted to take the exam rather than write the paper even after she insisted more take the final exam given the papers that she graded. The exams consisted of term identifications, short answer questions, and an essay. Since I wrote my answers by hand, I have no record of my responses for the final exam even though I earned an A. I do however, still have the questions and answers for my midterm on which I received 100%. Below is my essay response on my midterm.

<u>In class, we discussed the sister-wife stories (Genesis 12:10-20, Genesis 20, and Genesis 26:1-11). Choose one of the stories to be the earliest version of the story (composition not purported occurrence) and defend that choice, including why the other two stories came to stand alongside the original in the Bible and indicating important ways that the "later two" stories change the original.</u>

 Of the sister-wife stories in Genesis, the earliest version of the story is likely the one where Isaac and Rebekah are the main characters. The most glaring reason for this is that when all three narratives are examined, this is the only narrative (with Isaac) without blatant propaganda. The narrative with Isaac reads as a normal story about a man doing what he needs to survive and although Isaac lies about Rebekah being his sister it doesn't paint anyone in a bad light. As a result of famine, a normal occurrence in that part of the Near East given the agriculture, Isaac goes to Ge'rar. He lies about Rebekah being his sister but the king observed their behavior; this story isn't embellished with a divine intervention to warn or punish someone who is messing with Abraham's wife.

 Another major reason why it makes sense that this narrative comes first is that it contains the moment where the covenant is passed to Isaac. This is clear as God echoes things from the call of Abraham such as: going to a land God will show him, God will be with Isaac, giving all the lands to Isaac's seed, numerous offspring and finally that Isaac's offspring would be conduits through which all the nations of the earth would be blessed.

 The author tries to tie the narratives together by linking the famines of Abraham and Isaac. That said, there are great differences between the original and the other versions. The version from chapter 12 mentions the famine but Abraham is in Egypt instead of Ge'rar. Abraham prepares Sarai to lie to those who ask about their relationship but only Isaac lies in the version from chapter 26. In both other versions, the wife is actually taken with the version in chapter 12 having a sexual relationship between Pharaoh and Sarai but the chapter 20 version has none. Also, God punishes the kings in the other versions for taking Sarai (don't mess with Israel). In Isaac's version and chapter 20's version, the men give the king a reason for their deception although Isaac is straightforward and Abraham in chapter 20 is tried to be painted in a positive light by denying he is lying because Sarai was also his sister – so a half-truth perhaps or selective truth-telling.

As previously mentioned, propaganda is a big reason why the other versions were added to show that YHWH would stand up to anyone who offended His people. The other versions also are alongside Isaac's version for consistency and to show a common thread between the experiences of Abraham and Isaac. Lastly, the other version set the stage or provide reasons for the wealth of Abraham – that God blesses imperfect people.

Sermons

<u>Junior Year</u>

Faithfully grappling with the biblical text should inform all preaching. This is one of the primary lessons learned during my three courses in the art of preaching. Once again, as students we found ourselves learning what not to do as some of our worst habits became exposed under the wisdom of experienced practitioners of preaching. The first course taught by Dr. Ray McKenzie taught us the correlation method of preaching along with varying definitions for preaching. One of such definitions was provided by Phillips Brooks who defined preaching as "truth through personality." In addition, this course taught us the proper relationship between the preaching moment and the worship service. Dr. McKenzie taught us about liturgy and how each part of the service should aim toward proclaiming the same singular message. The scripture and prayer along with the songs in worship should agree with the subject of the sermon. To test our competence in this area, Dr.

McKenzie divided the class into groups with each group being expected to put together a complete worship service. For my group's service, I provided the prayer, written beforehand as Dr. McKenzie encouraged us to do, which reflected what we had been taught on February 27, 2010. This course also required that we write reaction papers to our weekly chapel services where we evaluated those worship services through the lens of what was taught by Dr. McKenzie.

As it would be in other courses, Dr. McKenzie called on us to critique the sermons of others. This was never for the purpose of public crucifixion or embarrassment but only for the purpose of edification that we all might learn from each other's successes and failures, each other's positives and negatives. This practice still stays with me. I cannot help but to critique and evaluate sermons that I hear. However, my motivation for listening closely is not to assign feedback or to determine whether or not they "flunked," rather it is to evaluate them for the purposes of my own edification, and to examine them for practices, techniques, or skills with which I would like to amend my own preaching practice.

Critiques in that class focused on the content of the sermons and also on the method of delivery. One of the pieces of advice given to us by other students was to simply read from the paper. Classmates and the professor reiterated to us that this was not church: there would be no whooping, no extravagant performance, no extra pre-sermonic prayers, and the list goes on. Flubs in this moment included a student asking someone else to read his scripture, a sermon focusing on the nakedness of Bathsheba that seemed to imply that he wished he was on that rooftop, and another whooping as if he was in church.

However, on the positive end, this class taught me much about the power of the sermonic moment. Listening to classmates including the writer of the foreword, Dr. David A. Jones, and Rev. Lucy Robertson challenged me to step up my game. In addition, arrogantly I assumed that while God could use anybody, that God would not use just anybody to do great things. Imagine my surprise when a classmate, who identified and identifies as a lesbian, preached a message about this treasure we have in earthen vessels with so much power and precision, that it shut the class down. This taught me that even if someone believes homosexuality to be sinful, one cannot state with any confidence that any such things disqualify us for service. If that were the case, all of us would be disqualified.

When it was my turn to deliver my sermon, nervousness overwhelmed me, but I focused on Dr. McKenzie's instructions to simply read from the paper and to resist the urge to perform for my peers. The sermon that I preached focused on the widow at Nain, who after losing her husband, is on her way to burying her only son before Jesus intervenes. My organizing observation or statement that demonstrated the good news of the text was this: "There are times when things go from bad to worse, but when such times occur God is near enough to help us and his power can and will turn things around." Upon finishing Dr. McKenzie looked at me and told me that I could take my seat as he had no criticism for my sermon. To me then and now, his silence in the area of criticism spoke volumes. Below is the entirety of this message.

"Hope for a Deteriorated Existence" - Luke 7:11-17

I.   Introduction

Most have us have seen medical shows on TV like "House" where each episode focuses on the deteriorating condition of a patient - the patient's condition was bad but soon the patient's condition has gone from bad to worse. This sounds similar to our common existence and experience where things sometimes deteriorate. On Sunday, July 16, 2006 at 11:26 PM, my son was born. The only problem is that according to my wife's doctor he wasn't supposed to be born until October 7th. He was born with all types of difficulties and I felt completely helpless. Things were bad. The following Friday I heard from a college friend who, after congratulating me, informed me that our mutual best friend had committed suicide. In five days things went from bad to worse. In hindsight, nothing but the power and proximity of God kept me from drowning in the pool of my own misery. Brothers and sisters, the truth of the matter is that there are times in life where things go from bad to worse; when such conditions prevail, God is near enough to comfort us and His power can and will turn things around.

II.   Circumstances deteriorated (vs. 12)

Jesus had just finished healing a centurion's servant from a distance when he went toward Nain in order to give a weeping widow a close encounter with the power of God. It is ironic that Jesus went into the city along with a large crowd that was most likely pleased about His ability to restore life when they encountered another large crowd coming out of the city, a funeral procession, which was coming to grips with death. The text tells us that this woman lost her husband and then in the text her only son had died – things were already bad and they got worse. After death had taken the men in her life she would be reduced to living a life reliant on the charity of others since she had no men to provide for her. This is on top of the fact that her family was already poor; and this is understood based on the fact that this dead man is not in an expensive coffin but rather lying on a bier or a stand. She didn't ask to be in this position and often times our quality of life declines and it is completely out of our control. How many of us have been in the position where it feels like when it rains it pours? Sometimes life leads us to become so cynical that we ascribe to Murphy's Law which states that "if anything can go wrong, it will." Our quality of life sometimes deteriorates but the good news is that help isn't far away.

III.   Closeness of Christ (vs. 11)

If Jewish custom would not have stated the necessity of burying the dead miles outside of the city, this woman would have never run into Jesus and this speaks to the providential timing of God. In this woman's darkest hour, the Light was near. This woman was in the very shadow of death but a shadow cannot exist without light and the Light was in the vicinity of this devastated woman. Soon this woman would see that she had no need to fear anything including evil because Jesus, the Emmanuel or "God with us" mentioned in the book of Isaiah, was with her. In other words, Jesus' proximity to the widow symbolizes that God is near in our time of distress and that God is a very present help in the time of trouble.

IV.   Compassion for the condition (vs. 13)

Next the text informs us that Jesus noticed her and then had compassion on this widow's condition. This speaks to the fact that God is not indifferent to the suffering of His children. After noticing her, in His compassion, Jesus comforted her and told her not to weep and by this He acknowledged her condition. The first part of his compassion is his feeling of deep sympathy and sorrow for this widow who was stricken by misfortune. Jesus told her to stop weeping before He did anything else. Jesus addressed her condition before He addressed the circumstances of her existence that brought her to this condition. He dealt with her before He dealt with it. Her condition was a symptom and her tears a symbol of her deteriorated existence. No matter the manifestation of a decline in the quality of life the good news is that somebody cares. Jesus was compassionate because He cared and also because He desired to change things by alleviating her suffering as we'll see next in the text.

V.   Corrected Existence (vs. 14-17)

The next thing we see in the text is that the power of God is used to correct her existence. In this passage Luke introduces his gentile audience to the only true God who has the power to turn things around. Notice that the text doesn't say anything about what the widow said or did to indicate her faith in Jesus' ability to turn her situation around. This tells us that sometimes the power of God intervenes independently of the exercise of faith because of the goodness of God. In these times God steps in to show you that it's not over until He says it's over. In the account, Jesus came forward and touched the bier and became ceremonially unclean. In other words He willingly humbled Himself for the purpose of changing this person's life just like He did for us. Then the bearers of the bier made no further movements to the grave site and Jesus resurrected this young man and burial was no longer necessary. In this passage Jesus raised someone from the dead for the first time and this helps us to understand that just because you haven't seen or heard God do something before doesn't mean that God is incapable of doing it. The text tells us that all it took was a word. The word of the Word was sufficient to raise this man from dead. That sounds like what God did; God sent the Word to help mankind regain the relationship that it lost because of sin. By doing what He did, Jesus gave this woman and other witnesses hope for when things go from bad to worse and gave her a reason not to give up. His actions encouraged or put courage into them to fight on. After this miracle was performed the pericope states that the people glorified God and according to the Greek they spread the word about Jesus all around the neighborhood. They gave credit where credit was due and spread the good news about what God had done through Christ. This is what we need to do: give God the glory and tell the old story.

VI.   Conclusion

In this text Jesus brought hope to this widow's deteriorated existence and turned things around because He was close, He cared, and He was compassionate enough to change things. My son is doing fine and I've overcome the grief in dealing with my friend who passed and so for me God turned things around. If you find yourself in the midst of a deteriorated existence God can and will do the same for you. It may not happen on this side of Jordan; God may turn things around in this life or end your suffering by taking you home to heaven but one way or another God will turn things around. God is omnipotent, omniscient and omnipresent – that means that He's able, He knows how and He's in position to turn things around. Like the widow in the text, God used Jesus to initiate a course correction for all of mankind in His precise and providential timing. When the fullness of time was come God sent Jesus because God can resurrect anything with a word. Dr. Kinney said that we celebrate Christmas right after the winter solstice and it reminds us that in man's darkest hour God sent the Light. We were dead in sins and trespasses but yet to be buried when Jesus interrupted our funeral procession. If you're saved, then you know for yourself that the infiltration of "I Am" into your life is what turned your life around. Based on this collateral you can know that no matter how dark your despair, the Light lives and our hope lives with Him so it's never over for us. So in the words of the Psalmist, even when things decline, "hope in God" and you can say "I will yet praise Him because He is my help and my God." One song says: "When in your way seems dark an' drear, you don't have to worry cause God is near; if in your heart there is no song, just keep the faith an' keep holding on; turn your face down, fast and pray, Jesus will always make a way; there's a bright side somewhere." We need to tell the world that there is hope for a deteriorated existence and His name is Jesus.

Middler Year

Dr. James Henry Harris possesses a distinguished reputation as an academic, preaching professor and a lecturer in the art of preaching. His expertise edified each of us as he taught us using his unique style. He served as my preaching professor during my middler year of seminary as the seminary rebuilt each of us. While Dr. McKenzie's class focused on the correlation method, Dr. Harris' class focused on teaching use the Hegelian dialectic of biblical preaching as practiced with excellence by the namesake of our school of theology, Dr. Samuel DeWitt Proctor. In this method, the antithesis (or the real) is juxtaposed against the thesis (or the ideal). In this method, the content of the text could provide either or both the antithesis and thesis, and the tension leads to a relevant question that must be answered by the text. The text's answers to this question constitute the synthesis or the body of the sermon.

In addition to this method, much of the class focused on properly interpreting texts and to that end, Dr. Harris assigned various non-religious readings that tested our ability to arrive at the correct interpretations of the text. Such readings included *Interpretation Theory* by Paul Ricoeur, as well as *Metamorphosis & Other Stories*, *The Stranger*, and *A Lesson Before Dying*. One of the lasting lessons that remains with me is that in biblical interpretation for sermonic purposes, the meaning of the text is in front of the text and that failing to do so will make it more difficult if not impossible for hearers to connect the preacher's subject with the preacher's chosen text. Dr. Harris repeated such notions during his lectures at the Hampton University Ministers Conference years later while representing STVU well.

For our sermons, Dr. Harris required that each of our sermons would come from the book of Psalms and we had to choose from a preselected list of texts. As it was with Dr. McKenzie's class, students were expected to provide critiques to our peers' sermons for our edification.

In the context of critiques, this class introduced us to the phrase "you have helped us"—meaning thank you for showing us what not to do. Once again, the skills exhibited by gifted preachers in that class, including Dr. Phillip Pointer, aided in my development as a preacher as it pushed me to be greater. I received no critiques during class, but on my printed sermon Dr. Harris said "Nick, continue to work hard on method and textual development. Good job! A-." The text that I chose and the sermon I wrote follows.

Text: Psalm 89:20-33 NRSV
Title: The Enduring Love and Faithfulness of God

Proposition

God is actively engaged in displaying God's faithfulness and enduring love for us.

Antithesis

We live in a society where it seems many people do not desire to be both loving and faithful. Shows such as Maury and Cheaters were created to expose and in some ways glorify the lack of faithfulness and sincere love in today's culture. Also in our society, individuals are thrown away or treated as expendable including children by people who demonstrate the antithesis of true love and faithfulness. We speak of love as an unselfish affection for someone else that leads us to choose to make sacrifices on his or her behalf. Being faithful is not allowing others or our selfishness and irresponsibility to compromise the integrity of what should be committed and loving relationships. Love and faithfulness are two sides to the same coin.

Thesis

In our text however we see that God is one who yet abides faithful and loving toward us and that is God. God personifies the love and faithfulness that we have discussed. God is the prototype for responsible parenting where God only acts for our edification. God does not throw us away in our vulnerability or abandon us at our worst but persists with us so we can become our best. The Psalmist in our text recounted the terms of the Davidic covenant and the author stressed the enduring faithfulness and love of God about every four or five verses. Our text today provides evidence that leads to the ideal verdict provided in verses 34-37: God's love and fidelity endure.

Relevant Question

The relevant question is: how does God demonstrate God's steadfast love and faithfulness to us?

Synthesis

First, the text tells us that God demonstrates God's enduring faithfulness and love by taking us from the call to victory. Verse 20 tells us that David, like each of us, was anointed or set apart or called to walk in God's purpose to be king. Verse 21 promises David access to God's power as both the hand and arm symbolize strength. This strength makes possible the victory described in verses 22 through 24. In verse 22 through 23, the text says that David's enemies would not be able to defeat him because God was on his side. God demonstrates God's love and faithfulness to us by protecting us from our enemies and by being the brains and brawn behind our victory. God is not intimidated by our opposition. God can help us overcome any resistance that lies between where we are and where God has purposed for us to go. God is able to ensure our transition from simply being called to becoming called conquerors. If you do not believe me, almost two years ago many of us started a process after being called to this place but God willing in May we will transition from just being called to being called victors. Verse 24 tells us that it is in God's name that David's horn would be exalted. In other words God deserves the glory for one's strength being exalted or the victory that one enjoys. God takes us from call to victory.

Secondly, the text shows us that God demonstrates God's steadfast love and fidelity by enabling our expansion and elevation. In Verse 25 once again the hand is symbolic of power. The New Living Translation describes the sea as the Mediterranean and the rivers as the Tigris and Euphrates with the implication that one has control over what one has between his or her hands. In other words God promised to extend David's territory and give David dominion.[29] God exhibits God's affection and fidelity when God grants us expansion and dominion over that which we did not previously control. In verse 26, God said that David will be compelled to point the finger at God and say that God is his God, Father and the Rock of his salvation. David would be compelled to give God the glory for his expansion. When God grants expansion we need to give credit where credit is due. But God also enables our elevation. In verse 27, the text says that God promised David that he would be the firstborn which was a place of privilege, inheritance, and promotion. God also promised that David's throne would be the highest of all the kings of the earth. This verse speaks to elevation. God can put us in places to which we could not ascend on our own just like God did with David. If God could elevate a shepherd boy to this throne, surely God can elevate us. Expansion and elevation are possible because according to verse 28 God's commitment to David would stand firm or not lose its footing. The good news is that God's commitment to us is not slipping in the least. God expands and elevates.

Lastly God demonstrates that God is still faithful and still loving toward us by ensuring that our relationship with God has staying power. In verse 29, God promised that David's line would be established forever and then provides evidence to support this notion in the next few verses. In verse 30 through 32 God promised to chastise David's descendants in the event that they end up disobedient to God's directives. God loves those affected by our relationship to the extent that God will correct them but not betray or abandon us. Verse 33 tells us that God will not allow David's descendants to undermine God's commitment to David. Staying power is possible because God makes our relationship and God's promises tamper proof for others. The text says "but." God is saying to us that 'when others who are connected to you and affected by what I've promised fail me I will not fail you.' It affects them but they can't affect it. Where one might expect others' behavior to poison our relationship with God, God's persistent love and faithfulness are the antidote. God gives our relationship with God staying power. But the ultimate evidence or demonstration of God's persistent love and faithfulness is the Christ event. God's faithfulness and love endure!

Senior Year

Our senior preaching class was special for several reasons. One of these reasons is due to our instructor Rev. Nathan Dell who possessed such a way with words. He inspired us to be more poetic in our preaching while also teaching us the application method. In the application method, the focus lies on making the word come alive by stressing its practical implications in our sermons. Preaching using this method should remain textual but should dig into the details that answer the question of "how?" Rev. Dell provided samples of this model in action including his eulogy of the late great preacher and preaching professor at STVU Dr. Miles Jerome Jones.

Another element which added to the uniqueness of this course included the fact that the course required each of us to write and preach two sermons in class: a special event sermon (selected from a provided list of topics i.e. Mother's Day, Easter, etc.) and a senior sermon. This course focused on the book of Proverbs so that each of our sermons' texts came from this book of wisdom. We had a great time in this class, which was the only class that required more than one sermon. Some of the persons involved in my previous publications, persons mentioned in this work, and some of my great friends—Rev. Dr. Eric Baldwin, Rev. Shamara Haynes, Rev. Monica Teal, Rev. Dr. Vonda Batts, Rev. Willitta Hawkins, Rev. Carolyn Taylor, Rev. H. Patrick Cason, Rev. Sam Warren, Rev. Darrell Hairston, Rev. Joshua King and others—preached strongly in this class. King had a different section, so his class was on another day, but I remember him telling the story of Rev. Dell's critique of one student who dragged Jesus into his sermon kicking and screaming. Rev. Dell would tell us that we should not strain ourselves trying to tie Jesus into every sermon—particularly Old Testament sermons. On this occasion, Rev. Dell told the student that while he preached, Jesus was walking around the classroom protesting. Rev. Dell had a way with words!

When the time came, I preached my special event sermon. The only critique that I can recall is being advised by the teaching assistant, Rev. Carla Jackson, Esq. to remain on the mountaintop by letting the sermon end with the Christ event and resurrection instead of going back down into practical application. She leveled this critique for my first sermon, but I do not remember any critiques for my senior sermon. When it came to my special event sermon, I wanted to be challenged (not that I believed that any of the topics was easy). Prior to this course I had never written a funeral sermon or a sermon that really challenged me emotionally. So, I chose to write my special event sermon on the funeral of a murdered child. I leveraged all I had been taught in that moment and produced a sermon of which I am still very proud. I preached that sermon, which the professor and other students received well before preaching my senior sermon later in the term. My senior sermon ironically could also serve as a fitting sermon for a funeral. I present these sermons for your reading below.

Special Event Sermon
Funeral of a Murdered Child
Proverbs 11:30-31 NRSV

We are here to remember this child who has been taken from our midst due by the violence of another. There is arguably no issue that can arouse our anger more than the idea of our children suffering. There are those among us who are not only sad for the loss but there are those among us who are likely angry because of how this loss came to be. However, we should cling to the good times and the positive memories of this child. This child has made an impression as will all of us. While we honor this child's memory we also must wonder where we go from here. But there is something in the text that can help us lead our lives more carefully. You should honor this child's memory by making wise lifestyle choices. Why should you make wise lifestyle choices?

You should make wise lifestyle choices because your lifestyle choices affect more persons than just you. In verse 30, the text reads that the fruit of the righteous is a tree of life and violence takes away lives. We see the principle of sowing and reaping. The harvest that results from an individual's sowing affects more people than that individual. The Tree of life is a poetic and metaphoric expression for life itself. The righteous life is the soil in which a tree of life takes root. It has the nutrients, fertility and means to promote the growth of a resource by which each of us, as well as others, can go on living. In other words, this part of the verse speaks to the fact that the quality of our lives improves because of righteous living but also that by bearing fruit others may eat of it and be blessed. It is bigger than us. Joseph is an example of this who because he was righteous he was positioned to be a blessing and to preserve life.

Not only is the fruit of the righteous a tree of live but conversely violence takes lives. For many of us, and not just in this particular case, we have experienced the sting of death initiated by violence. Violence is the act of inflicting harm upon in individual usually with the intent to do harm or with indifference to any harm that may come to that individual. There are various opinions as to how this verse should read. This is partially due to confusion about the Hebrew word that should be used. The Hebrew words for a wise person and violence are very similar. It makes sense however to contrast the righteous and the wicked and their relationships to the preservation of life. The former works to preserve it while the latter uses violence in order to take it away. While Proverbs 24:2 reads that plotting violence is characteristic of the wicked this does not mean that we should hate the violent. No amount of hatred is able to restore or produce life. We should not allow hatred to be sown in our hearts because this hatred fuel violent behavior.

In spite of the violence that took this child, let us remember this child and honor this child by living a life that this child would be proud of. How it ends is not more important than what came before the end. One day we will all leave behind a memory and we do not want the means of how we left to overshadow how others were blessed through our lives. When Martin Luther King Jr.'s name is mentioned our first thought is not often of the person that took his life but on what he gave us before leaving. He does not have a national memorial because of his death but due to the value of his life. So let it be with this child and all of us. Let us not only live for the moment but so that even in death, like the righteous Abel, we will yet have a voice. Even in death the voice of the righteous speaks through their legacies which are able to quicken succeeding generations. We want our legacies to give voice to the life we led.

Why should you make wise lifestyle choices? You should make wise lifestyle choices because your choices will come back to you. Verse 31 says that the righteous as well as the wicked and sinners are repaid according to their instances of wickedness. Oftentimes our lifestyle choices have a boomerang effect in that they will return and come back to haunt us. We all will reap. Since it will come back to others and ourselves, we should not seek retribution. We cannot control others' choices but we can choose not to seek retribution. We can choose to be angry without choosing to sin. We should not let the anger of what happened to this child or to us multiply our regrets. We should not seek revenge. Revenge is a dish that is best left unserved.

We should not seek revenge because as Martin Luther King Jr. once said "darkness cannot drive out darkness only light can do that." The memory is not honored by repeating the wickedness of those who have extinguished this child's flame. Exacting revenge only temporarily numbs the pain. This is because our pain is not about violent but about this precious child that we've lost to violence. In this case and others, we should be wise enough that we do not allow what others have done to us to consume us to the extent that we become obsessed with paying them back. We should realize that life will repay them. This is true because God's got it. Let God deal with it lest in our fervor to exact revenge we put God in a position where God has to deal with us also. God is not mocked – whatever a person sows a person will reap. Vengeance is mine, I will repay saith the Lord. In other words, we serve a just God. When someone has wronged us, we need to be willing to trust their fate to God's hands and trust God to do what should be done. It is good news to know that in our suffering, God is yet with us and can grant us peace while we await justice.

Like others who have been taken from this world through violence, this child's memory yet lives on. Not only that but many of us can say that we have been saved because of a memory. It is a memory of one righteous person's life in particular that gives life to all those that embrace it. There is no greater example of a tree of life than that produced by the righteous life of Jesus Christ. He came that we would have life and have it more abundantly. We have been saved because of the work and persistent memory of One who met His end through violent means. Jesus suffered violence at the hands of the wicked who crucified Him. Jesus asked God to forgive those at whose hands He died. But this righteous man yet lives and because He lives we have access to the tree of life. He's the righteous gift who keeps on giving. Jesus is evidence that even after violence humbles, God is able to exalt. Leave the justice to a just God. Walk with God, and let God comfort and keep you in this hour only as God can.

Senior Sermon
"Reasons to Live Righteously"
Proverbs 10:7

Memories are powerful things. A memory is a unit of recollection surrounding people, places, things or events. During our sojourn in this space memories have been developed. Now we will be able to look back upon the times that we were able to laugh together as well as engage in critical thinking, intense debate and discovery. We will remember Dr. Harris' accusations of sermons or outlines taking the class to the very gates of hell. We will remember Dr. Jackson's idiosyncrasies, Dr. Bond's discernment, Dr. Kim's wit, Dr. McKenzie's "what," Dr. Gould-Champ's candor, Dr. Kinney's passion, Dr. Young's charm and Reverend Dell's poetic inclinations. However, the memories that we've made in this place ultimately will not matter more to this world than how we individuals have made a difference. This is because as this text reminds us for every life lived a legacy is left behind. We may not leave behind a fortune for our heirs but all of us will leave behind a name. Our names are and will be connected to the memories that have been engraved onto the minds of those we have influenced. The text is a pushback against the thinking of the writer of Ecclesiastes who wrote that all is vanity in that it helps us to see that our lives after we have lived them do not have to be worthless.[30] The author of this text connected the prospect of a person's remembrance with that person's lifestyle. By focusing on the remembrance of those who have lived, the aim of this passage is to get us to focus on our lifestyles with the understanding that lifestyles become legacies. Knowing this, it is important for you to live righteously. But why is it important for you live righteously?

It is important for you to live righteously so that your legacy does not become worthless. The second part of verse 7 reads that the name of the wicked will rot. This is not talking about instances of wickedness but a slant in lifestyle toward the things that are not of God. In this portion of the verse the emphasis is on the name of the wicked. A name is more than some combination of consonants and vowels that collaborate to label us. It points to our individual reputations which in death become part of our legacies. Reputation is a perception of one's character with the concession that only God knows our true character; it is an assumption about who we are based on what we did or have been rumored to do. Notice the fate of the name or memory of the wicked: it will rot. Notice the tense of this part of the text: the name of the wicked "*will* rot". It suggests that the wicked may be here today but that their names will rot or decay in the future. Rotting is a strong characterization of this probability. When something rots it decomposes. Usually there are two characteristics of that which is rotting - the stench and the negative prognosis of the subject's staying power.

The fact that rotting produces a stench helps us to see that the wicked are remembered but the smell of their memory offends the senses. It is not simply an unpleasant odor but that which is capable of turning the stomach. Most of us could admit that while not pretending to be perfect we have encountered such wickedness in others to the extent that to look back upon it makes us sick. This includes persons who have taken advantage, assaulted or abused you and the very mention of their name makes you queasy. This is why even after we forgive persons for what they have done to us we may not be able to stand their company because their wickedness makes us nauseous. Rotting is a continual process and the more time elapses the worse the smell gets and it takes away from the quality of life of those who experience it. This explains how persons can express that others are "dead" to them. When you say that someone is dead to you what you are really saying is that their existence is so detrimental to your own happiness that you treat them as if they are rotten or rotting in your presence and you cannot stand the smell.

The negative prognosis for the endurance of that which is rotting suggests that eventually its existence will come to nothing. This reflects the likelihood that those who died in wickedness lived their lives to some extent in vain because their memories are worthless to those who remember them. History is filled with people whose names are considered irrelevant because people desire to contract a specific form of amnesia and forget that these persons ever existed because of their wickedness. I believe this is what the writer of Job had in mind when he wrote that "Their memory perishes from the earth, and they have no name in the street."[31] As the names of the wicked deteriorate, their names are only mentioned as a matter of fact and raised as a part of history so that persons can avoid following their examples. However, we should desire that the memory of our lives serve as more than just cautionary tales like that of Bin Laden, Gadhafi and other wicked persons who will not be missed. These are those whose only contribution to succeeding generations is a model of what not to do and who not become.

Why is it important for you to live righteously? It is important for you to live righteously so that your legacy will benefit others. The text reads in the first part of verse 7 that the memory of the righteous is a blessing or the source of a blessing. In other words, those who recall the lives of the righteous somehow benefit from doing so. The righteous or just are those who live a life pleasing to God. For contrary to the poor reputation of the wicked, God knows and approves of the character of the righteous. For there is no separation between behavior and character; you are what you do. All of us should live in a way that compels God to say amen to our lives. According to the text, this amen is echoed by those the righteous leave behind when they consider their memories. Like the wicked, people remember the righteous but the notion that this memory is a blessing suggests that others embrace the legacies the righteous leave behind.

The memory of the righteous benefits those who have access to the memory. In contradistinction to recollections surrounding the wicked, the memory of the righteous ought to add meaning and joy to the lives of those who remember them. Notice that this portion of the verse says "*is* a blessing" or that others are likely to be blessed in the present for the lives the righteous led in the past. It implies a sense of perpetual blessing whenever persons remember the lives of the upright. This means that you have something to live for; all of us should live today not simply for the moment but also in order to benefit those who come after us. This brings to mind the sacrifices of those who waged a righteous struggle for civil rights and in doing so knowingly sacrificed themselves for a cause that would benefit the generations that followed.

Remembering the righteous can benefit the living because the life of the righteous can be a template that others may follow in order to live a life that is similarly approved by God. When people remember how we lived to please God and how we overcame trials and temptations they can be blessed. When those by whom we are survived remember that we learned from our mistakes and that our living aligned with that which we both taught and proclaimed they can be blessed. When our heirs reminisce about the times we shared wisdom and our testimonies they can be blessed. When those who we leave behind recall our persistent effort in search of truth and our walk in integrity they can be blessed. They can be blessed by these memories because they provide evidence of God's faithfulness and evidence to the premise that living for God in these times is still plausible. They can be blessed by these memories because they may inspire them to win their own battles and overcome their own obstacles. They can be blessed by these memories because through our example they can see that with God nothing is impossible.

I can confidently say that many of us would not be here had it not been for the legacies of righteous men and women who came before us including the namesake of our school Dr. Samuel DeWitt Proctor. Their memories bless us still. Also, the fact that Dr. Miles Jones could be eulogized truthfully with the message "A Prince and a Great Man" testifies to the fact that he was a righteous man whose memory is still a blessing. You should want the same thing to be said about you. We should want our legacies to be so expansive that they cannot be easily summarized on our epitaphs. At least, however, let it be said of us what was said of Enoch that we had the testimony that we pleased God. We can do this because one righteous man's life has been a blessing to generations.

To the point of the text, we think less and less of Judas the further we get from his betrayal in Gethsemane and his name is still rotting but we are still blessed by the memory of the One he betrayed. The memory of what Jesus did blesses us still. The gospels tell the story of his precious memory and we are blessed by his memory because he showed us what God wanted from humanity. His memory is a blessing right now because when I remember how he fed the families of 5000 men I'm blessed to know that God can supply my needs. His memory is a blessing right now because when I remember how he healed the demoniac I'm blessed to know that God can help me overcome my issues and exorcise my demons. His memory is a blessing right now because when I remember how he healed the woman with an issue of blood I'm blessed to know that God can mend my brokenness and give me a new lease on life.

But ultimately the memory that stands out the most is the reason why he has a name that is above every name. For in spite of the confusion and lack of resolution in my Christology I'm still confident that He was wounded for my transgressions and bruised for my iniquities. If memory serves me correctly He died on an old rugged cross. If memory serves me correctly He was put in a borrowed tomb. If memory serves me correctly early Sunday morning God raised him from the dead. His memory is the reason that there is a name I love to hear, I love to sing its worth; it sounds like music in my ear, the sweetest name on earth. O how I love Jesus because he first loved me and gave himself for me. Wherefore God has highly exalted him and given him a name that is above every name that at the name of Jesus every knee should bow and every tongue confess that He is Lord.[32] O magnify the Lord with me and let us exalt His name together.[33]

Conclusion

My time in seminary forever altered the ways in which I encounter and engage with the text both for the purposes of sermon preparation and study. I am forever grateful for how my professors poured into me and equipped me with tools that I did not have before coming to seminary. These sermonic assignments stretched me in some ways, and I am grateful for the wakeup call I received in my biblical studies course. I consult with these tools frequently in my current assignment and look forward to future success after being so effectively equipped by courses and assignments that led me to wrestle with the text. I am glad that when it came to being empowered to preach more effectively and be faithful to the biblical text, I trusted the process.

[1] Coogan, 93 NT.
[2] Brand, 1057.
[3] Mills, 531.
[4] Brand, 1057.
[5] Brown, 675.
[6] Brand, 1057-1058.
[7] Soulen, 202-203.
[8] Mills, 531.
[9] Coogan, 94-95 NT.
[10] Harrelson, 1862.
[11] Brown, 692.
[12] Gorman, 98.
[13] Brown, 692.
[14] Wenell, 4p.
[15] Mills, 508.
[16] Mills, 508.
[17] Mills, 626.
[18] Coogan, 60 NT.
[19] Mills, 509.
[20] Loader, 56.
[21] Coogan, 105 NT.
[22] Brand, 1025.

²³ Brown, 692.
²⁴ Coogan, 18 NT.
²⁵ Coogan, 60 NT.
²⁶ Harrelson, 1808.
²⁷ Brown, 692.
²⁸ King Jr., Martin Luther. "Pilgrimage to Nonviolence." Fellowship 24 (Sep. 1958): 4-9.
²⁹ Matthew Poole, *A Commentary on the Holy Bible.* Vols. Volume II: Psalms-Malachi. III vols. (Peabody, MA: Hendrickson, 1985), 141.
³⁰ Ecclesiastes 1:2 KJV.
³¹ Job 18:17 NRSV.
³² C.f. Philippians 2:9-11 KJV.
³³ Psalm 34:3 KJV.

2

Historical

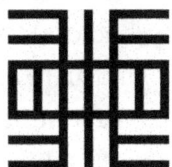

To this day, my courses taken in seminary in church history remain my favorites. These courses led me to fall in love with church history as we learned about the ways in which the church and modern theology evolved since the New Testament times. Adam Bond, Ph.D. served as our professor and he was one of the main reasons for the effectiveness and enjoyment of the course. He not only taught us about pivotal persons and moments in church history from the New Testament to modern times, but he also empowered us with the ability to argue. Through multiple papers, he challenged us to decipher, extend, and even construct original arguments. In some cases, we argued against our own beliefs which further aided in our ability to be able to argue. At the time, I did not understand how these exercises and assignments would assist me in taking the GRE exam in preparation for a Ph.D. program. While pursuing a Doctor of Ministry degree instead due to uncertainty about residency, Dr. Bond encouraged me to know that I possessed the ability to complete a Ph.D. In the two courses in church history, I earned perfect or nearly perfect scores in part due to my photographic memory but also due to my affection for the subject matter.

These classes awakened my love of origin stories. Studying the origins of the church to include the heavy influences of African theologians such as Augustine had a profound impact upon me. I loved hearing and reading about the shaping of the church from the days of the diaspora due to persecution to modern times. This new love of origin stories shows in my attraction to biographies, documentaries, and other programs that cover diverse subjects to include sports, entertainment, and religious figures. As a result, oftentimes, I watch interviews of entertainers on YouTube or gravitate toward articles that cover persons' journeys to prominence. In my doctoral program, I read the biography of the great mystic Howard Thurman after reading Samuel DeWitt Proctor's biography during my first stint in seminary. My newfound love of stories also explains my attraction to the Storytime component of the IC3 Church Conference where respected church leaders share about the pitfalls of ministry and their journeys in general.

Argumentative Papers

Below one will find my six argumentative papers with the first three from my first semester of Church History followed by the remaining three from my second semester. Each semester follows the same order of analysis, position, and then finally reflection. They include papers that required students to decipher arguments in order to describe them, extend them, or arrive and build original arguments ourselves. The hope is that one might see an evolution in my ability to argue, extend arguments, and decode arguments. One of these papers focuses on a paper written by Dr. Martin Luther King, Jr. during his time in seminary, which served as an inspiration for this volume. His position or depth of thought is consistent with the picture of Dr. King during seminary as chronicled in the book *The Seminarian* by Patrick Parr. The position papers on subjects such as the nature of Christ sparked spirited debate in class. Dr. Bond was very skillful in deciphering and then undermining the arguments made by students in class, and this forced us to develop stronger arguments and to reason our arguments through.

Analysis Paper - *Letter to the Magnesians* by Ignatius of Antioch

Ignatius, also called Theophorus, was the bishop of Antioch who wrote letters to churches while being transported on his way to Rome to be martyred during the rule of the Roman emperor Trajan (98-117). Ignatius' letters reflected the fact that there were those who claim to be a part of the Christian movement but who did not agree with the traditional understanding of the apostles' teachings (WCM, pg. 72). This is one such missive.

Ignatius argued that the church of Magnesia needed to preserve unity in the church. Ignatius made his case as he explained that it was the unity between Jesus and the Father that enabled Jesus to fulfill his mission, he wrote that the church should be unified under the leadership that is an extension of God's authority, and suggested that these Christians at Magnesia should be unified with the Godhead and each other. Ignatius argued that there should be unity in the church of the Magnesians based upon the unity that existed from eternity between the Lord and the Father. Ignatius reasoned that just as the Lord did nothing without the Father because they were united, so the church should work in unity with the leaders of the church.

Ignatius argued that the Magnesians should be unified with their leadership, which included the bishop, presbyters and deacons, and this unity should be characterized by obeying this leadership. The words that Ignatius used to describe these persons reflect his respect for these offices and reflected the fact that he expected the Magnesians to honor these leaders. Ignatius suggested that the authority of bishops and of leaders was derived from God and that God led those leaders. This is evident from part VI where Ignatius stressed harmony with God and how the Magnesians were to follow the bishop as if they were following God and the presbyters as if they were following the apostles. He further noted that to offend them was to offend the God that supported them. The Magnesians were exhorted to listen to the leadership and obey them lest their rebellion cause disunity in the church and not reflect the virtue of unity that characterizes Christianity. Ignatius' argument for the preservation of unity is further supported by the argument that the Magnesians need to be unified with the Godhead which should be evidenced by their harmony and conformity with God. He also later reasoned the Magnesians should follow the example of the prophets who were unified through the Spirit with Christ because there was no life for them apart from the Godhead. Ignatius argued that the prophets suffered but were faithful because they possessed a union with the Godhead. So, Ignatius suggested that the Magnesians' suffering in some respects evidenced a connection with God and so he appealed to them to preserve this connection. The implication is that just as Jesus raised the prophets from the dead and this testified of their faithfulness, that God would someday honor the Magnesians' persevering faith and attachment. Lastly, the writer argued that the Christian believers at Magnesia needed each other and this included the aforementioned leadership. Ignatius asked the church to pray for him and other believers and relayed a greeting from the Ephesians. For him, all of these things highlighted the connection amongst Christians.

Ignatius' efforts to inform the church of Magnesia and others during his last days are commendable and he used his last moments to encourage unity in the church in spite of all the factors of that day which could have served to divide them. Ignatius is important to the history of the Christian church because his concept of a "monarchial Episcopal conception of the church had won out over the more egalitarian and charismatic forms of leadership reflected in the Didache" by the end of the second century through the doctrine communicated in his letters (WCM, pg. 62). This document is relevant today for its instruction in the necessity for Christians to be unified and in how the members of the church should not let anything divide them. While the suggestion to follow church leadership is commendable, I disagree with the notion of blindly following any leader other than God since no Christian believer, even a bishop, is infallible.

Position Paper – *On Nature and Grace* by Augustine of Hippo

Augustine of Hippo (354-430) lived during "a time of spiritual and theological ferment in the West" (WCM, 231). However, Augustine's ideas surrounding original sin reflected a radical shift from the more acceptable position on the matter, at least to the Greek-speaking East, which was a "moderate doctrine of human responsibility and capacity to choose God" (WCM, 233). Augustine was correct in his work "On Nature and Grace" (415CE) where he argued that human beings wholly depend on the grace of God found in Christ for salvation that is an act of faith born out of the grace and mercy of God. He is correct because due to original sin human beings only deserve death, because human beings are incapable of fixing a sin defect that overwhelms them, and because it is impossible for human beings to earn salvation or eternal life.

As a result of original sin, all human beings regardless of age or background deserve death. Since there is no condemnation to them that are in Christ Jesus then logically this means that there must be condemnation for those who are without (John 3:18, Romans 8:3). Christ died for all because all were born into sin (John 3:16). The deserved penalty for both inherited and personal sin is death and it is God's mercy that holds back this penalty for all of mankind (Romans 6:23). Every human being since Adam has died because of this sin with Jesus being the only exception. While people in Augustine's context may have used their sin nature as an excuse, and this should have been addressed, Pelagius goes too far by asserting that there is no such thing as original sin. Clearly the offense of one, Adam, has brought condemnation to human race due to the inherited sinful nature and predisposition to sin of all descendants (Romans 5:12-14).

At the same time, human beings are incapable of doing anything to remedy a defect that overcomes them. Human beings are powerless to eradicate the root sickness of which personal sin is a symptom. In other words, humankind needs someone or something greater than itself to fix this problem. When people have a medical issue that they are powerless to fix oftentimes they visit someone who has credibility because this person has expertise and experience. For salvation, people need to reach back to God who has the credibility, expertise, experience and the power to fix what ails humankind. To argue that God would send Jesus simply to remedy individual sin suggests that Jesus is a very poor Physician who only seeks to address symptoms and not cure the illness. The ordinance of baptism is a public declaration by the baptized of a consultation with the Great Physician and an admission that there is someone greater than them. The recovery from original sin is similar to that of the Twelve Step Program for alcoholics who must first acknowledge that they are powerless over their addiction and then that there is a higher power than them. God sent mankind help as the result of God's grace because the blessings of salvation are impossible to earn. Jesus came in order for Christians to be new creations because the old creation with its old nature was insufficient to merit salvation. Jesus did not come to show the world the sufficiency of human nature because like Adam Jesus was born with a sinless nature and this is the only way for human beings to be able to keep the law. As a result, for humankind justice only lies in the help of the grace of Christ and so one's fate is determined based on one's acceptance of the gospel of Christ (Romans 5:1). In one particular Christmas season, my brother and I received gifts beyond our expectations – leather jackets and CD players – although we accomplished nothing that was especially worthy of recognition. This grace born out of love exhibited by my father and mother is similar to the parental grace that led God to give mankind a gift which it could never deserve: salvation.

Reflection Paper – *Teaching the Reformation in My Context*

One of the most effective methods for teaching any subject is to explain the subject by comparing it to terms and subjects familiar to the audience. To this end, using the Civil Rights Movement as a hermeneutical lens through which African American persons can view the Reformation is the best way to teach the subject of the Reformation to my largely African American congregation. This is because both of these subjects involved a movement of various elements, both involved a repudiation of a dominant entity, and both began as agitators sought to take away the task of identifying themselves from the dominant party.

First, both the Civil Rights Movement and the Reformation were movements which were not isolated to one singular event. These movements were both symptoms of a hidden deeper sickness or tension in their individual contexts. The Reformation came as the result of the social abuse and spiritual poverty of the people at least through the eyes of one of its progenitors Martin Luther. The Civil Rights Movement began in large part because of the social poverty of African Americans who were still not considered equal to the white majority. However, just as the Reformation had its social, political and religious aspects, the Civil Rights Movement was an effort to establish social and political equality and its foundation was laid on the principles of Christianity by arguing that the status quo was ungodly and unjust. Each of these movements came as the result of internal pressure designed to demand freedom by each era's oppressed. This information would aid my context in showing that effort to enact change must be persistent and that we cannot isolate ourselves in the practice of ministry and fail to address a holistic mission.

Each of the aforementioned movements involved a repudiation of a dominant entity that society at large accepted as the norm. In the context of the Reformation that dominant entity was the Catholic Church and those who stood in its way were largely swept aside by methods through brute force including through persecution and the crusades. The dominant entity during the era of the Civil Rights Movement was white supremacy. This bias manifested itself in the social, political and religious realms of this country and was reflected in Dr. Martin Luther King Jr.'s missive to white clergy in his "Letter From a Birmingham Jail". Key persons became responsible for initiating these movements and these persons believed that the establishment had to be rejected in favor of something better. In the face of dominance, these key persons were labeled as extremist by the dominant entities. These leaders furthered their cause based on their particular visions or dreams of what should be and did not let fear of the establishment keep them from giving themselves to making a difference. Like Jesus, these difference makers refused to hold their peace just to keep the peace. These leaders who were the voices of repudiation personified the words of Mahatma Gandhi that "we are the change we seek in the world." As a result, the practice of ministry in my context should therefore be a voice in the realm of social justice and give a voice to those who have not been heard.

The Reformation came about as the result of an effort of Christians to identify themselves apart from the Catholic Church and to own this definition, and this mirrors the Civil Rights Movement. As the dominant entity, it was the Catholic Church that sought to establish the identity of the Christian through its leadership including the papacy. The leaders of the reformation redefined the elements of Christian identity including appearance, doctrine and worship practices. In a similar vein, the Civil Rights Movement sought to establish an identity of the African American apart from the esteem of the white majority by painting the African American as a equal to the Anglo-Saxon American, and as a result, a joint-heir of the American Dream. Part of this was turning their race from being a point of shame to being a point of pride. Through these examples we can learn to be courageous enough not to let outsiders determine who we are in my setting and instead we need to minister in both an effective and authentic way.

Analysis Paper – *A Survey of the Summe of Church Discipline* by Thomas Hooker

Thomas Hooker (1586-1647) was an educated and influential Puritan who came to New England due to the persecution he faced as a leader of the Puritan party in the Church of England and his "thought commanded international attention" (SCT 47). In line with Hooker's other work, this work reflects the larger quest of Puritanism for a reformed church as Hooker used the words of this digest to articulate "his understanding of the elements constituting the church on earth" (Ibid.). His analysis of the church in scholastic categories reflected the larger Puritan emphasis on the theme of covenant, while also reflecting Hooker's context in the logical manner in which the topic of "biblical doctrine" was handled.

In chapters two and four of this work, Hooker argued that the integrity of the membership of the visible church must be preserved by limiting outside civil influence on membership, by restricting membership to the visible church based on persons' public examples, and by encouraging covenantal relationship and unity among the membership. Hooker articulated that civil authorities had no say with regard to the composition of the visible church and defended this based on the premise that Jesus is the head of the church and therefore the church primarily is a spiritual entity whose membership cannot be regulated by governmental authority. Also to this point, Hooker stated that the locality of persons in parishes determined by government did not automatically qualify a person for church membership because civil authority and the internal authority of the church occupied different domains. According to Hooker, keeping civil and spiritual matters separate was a key factor to retaining the integrity of the church.

Hooker further noted that only visible saints should comprise the membership of the visible church and this was one method of preserving the church's integrity. Hooker's argument was that a visible commitment to Christ should precede church membership instead of membership serving as a symptom of said commitment. He supported his case by stating that if membership of the visible church is open to those who are not already exemplifying their conversion and personal integrity, then the integrity of the visible church would be injured and it would be against the design of the founder of the church who is Christ. He pointed out that the church should be willing to enforce church discipline and remove those persons from the church who undermine its integrity and who by their actions no longer seem to be visible saints.

Fostering a covenantal relationship and unity among the saints, Hooker argued, would also ensure that the visible church retained its integrity. This is possible because, according to Hooker, the covenantal relationship encourages mutual accountability and unity among the membership is important as the saints either explicitly or implicitly set about to walk in the ways of Christ. Hooker argued that as the saints worked in covenant with one another and in unity with one another, that this would cause the visible church to maintain its substance and vitality, and its integrity by extension, as these efforts exemplify visible saints.

Hooker is important to the understanding of the history of Christianity in the United States because under his direction several ministers led settlers from Massachusetts to Connecticut and as a result they created one of four early colonies where Puritanism was the dominant religion (HCU 41). Hooker's work is relevant for today's context because some churches and their members are unwilling to do what is necessary in order to preserve the integrity of the church as a whole including the enforcement of church discipline. Ministerial greed and sexual transgressions among other things have injured the integrity of the visible church and so Hooker's work is necessary now so that the church may be steered back into being the church that Christ, the church's founder, intended. Also, many persons within the church today have forgotten the principles of covenant and unity, and refuse to contribute their effort and gifts toward the benefit of the members of the visible church thus undermining its integrity.

Position Paper – *Why King Was Right*

The exact nature of Christ has been debated for centuries. As Dr. Martin Luther King Jr. noted in his work "The Humanity and Divinity of Jesus", interested persons have often ascribed some level of both humanity and divinity to Jesus. King points out that while there has been debate about Jesus' humanity, many agree on the subject of Jesus' divinity but not in regard to when Jesus took on divinity. In King's work, he was correct when he argued that Jesus was completely human and divine but that his divinity was not inherently present in his incarnation. He is correct because Jesus experienced a life typical of other Biblical prophets who were human, and because Jesus' divinity came as the result of his unwavering reliance upon God.

By human, both King and I mean that Jesus was a complete human made of the same substance as us that the body of Jesus was not a phantasm as the Docetists believed. As a human being Jesus endured the unique human experience that still includes moral struggles and struggling with one's limitations. Jesus possessed foreknowledge and a mandate to represent God in the mold of other Biblical prophets who were also completely human and experienced the highs and lows of prophetic ministry and who needed periodic encouragement (Hebrews 1:1-2). In the pattern of other prophets, Jesus had to arise from among the people and he served as a prophet to all of humanity because he was a part of humanity. Also, Jesus expressed his humanity through his emotions similarly to other prophets through the shedding of tears, as King mentioned, and through righteous indignation (clearing the temple).

The other prophets' ministries were limited by time and space and so was Jesus' ministry. For example, Lazarus' sisters both echo the sentiment that if Jesus had been there that Lazarus would not have died and this is admittance from scripture that Jesus was not omnipresent and this is consistent with all human beings. In addition to the divine attribute of omnipresence, King uses as evidence of Jesus' humanity the fact that he was not omniscient. To this I would add as evidence of

Historical

Jesus' humanity the fact that Jesus was not omnipotent or possessive of all authority because if he were he would not have noted that he had been given all power in heaven and earth after his resurrection.

While Dr. King noted the otherness of Christ, his union with God was symptomatic of his dependence upon God. Throughout Jesus' life, Jesus openly received help from God including the receipt of the Holy Spirit at his baptism and the ministering he received from the angels. Jesus engaged in spiritual disciplines such as prayer and fasting in order to show devotion and a reliance on God for strength and courage. It was this reliance upon God that eventually led to Jesus being able to perform acts thought to be reserved for God including offering the forgiveness of sins. The wisdom with which Jesus ministered and discerned the needs of people came as the result of his dependence upon God. Also his ability to reinterpret the law according to the spirit of the law proved that he had a greater understanding of the Spirit behind the law than the masters of the law. In becoming so dependent upon God, Jesus became the ultimate revelation of God by being the embodiment of the will of God for all men to willingly become subject to God. Jesus was tempted but failed to yield to his temptation and did not sin. He was unwilling to rely on the pleasures of this world but chose rather to pledge allegiance to the will of God even laying down his life in pursuit of the will of God being fulfilled on earth as it is in heaven. As a Father, I find joy in seeing my children express their reliance upon me for what they need because their expressions are ones of faith, trust and confidence. Jesus was divine because he exemplified the faith, trust and confidence of a child in his parent and so provided evidence that God was in him just as the essence of a good father will be seen in his children. No one reflects the character of a parent more than that parent's child and this is yet true of Jesus who truly lived like he was his Father's son. King was right!

Reflection Paper – *The Role of Emotion in Christian Formation and/or Salvation*

Emotion is very important for both Christian formation and salvation. Oftentimes expressions of emotions are responses to a thought process related to the receipt and acceptance of some information whether this information is interpreted as good or bad. Knowing the role of emotion in Christian formation and salvation is important for my context so that it will understand how emotion aids in and follows salvation, how emotion helps Christians transition from salvation to holy living and how emotion if genuinely expressed will draw others to Christ.

Emotion is important both in receiving salvation and enjoying salvation because while sadness accompanies the realization that one cannot save oneself, joy comes when one accepts the notion that Jesus paid a debt of sin that no other individual could satisfy. Emotion should be more of an after effect to the logical processing of the gospel because as in other cases, such as hearing happy or sad news, an emotional response is dependent upon the belief in the veracity of this news. According to Ephesians 2:8 it is faith or belief and trust in God and the gospel that leads to salvation but one would have no emotional response to the gospel if one rejected the gospel as a lie. Phoebe Palmer frequently used scripture, such as Revelation 1:5-6 that discusses the bloody sacrifice of Christ, in her work "Entire Devotion to God" (1845) to elicit emotions of joy from the Christian readers who have already accepted the gospel as truth. This is important because a sincere emotional response of joy to the gospel reflects one's faith in the gospel.

Phoebe Palmer used scripture regarding the gospel in an effort for build a foundation for stressing the importance of holiness and sanctification (I Corinthians 5:19-20). She suggested that one's commitment to Christ may be deemed authentic based on the evidence of holy living and this transition from salvation to holiness is aided by emotion. She stated that holiness was the duty of every believer to attain and emotion further motivates Christians to fulfill this duty of being living sacrifices (SCT 175, Romans 12:1-2). Authentic emotion plays the role of affirming the faith on which holy living is based upon. It is possible that on Palmer's "day of days" her receipt of a deeper sense of the faith resulted in initial emotion after longing for such an experience and this preceded her effort to lead a holy life. It is natural to experience emotion upon receiving something that one has waited in agony for. Without the genuine emotion that accompanies the gratitude due to God for all that God has done, salvation could become a dead end road for some, where for them it does not appropriately lead to the holy living that Palmer champions. True gratitude to God leads to holy living. This information is vital for my context as we have seen numerous persons profess the acceptance of salvation but depart never to return in an effort to further be sanctified and formed, and who use salvation as a license to sin.

Authentic expressions of emotion within the church only aids the image of the church as being a place where persons are not afraid to be themselves and to be transparent. Also, others will be drawn to want to share in whatever it is that has caused such genuine and joyful expressions from Christians. Many times, especially in my context, persons including myself have been guilty of mindless worship or simply mimicking the emotions of others. It is not the failure to accept the gospel or the failure to acknowledge the need for further Christian formation that is the problem but rather it is the absence of thought and reflection that leads to the perception of the church being phony and insincere. When emotion is properly derived from deep thought people will more easily transition from simply being observers in my context to allowing God to shape them as God sees fit. When this happens, I contend that persons from outside of the church who are authentic and persons of character will be attracted to my local context and in the end strengthen the body. The privileges of church relation and salvation are worthy of emotional expression and this expression only reflects that the members of the church are rooted and grounded in the faith.

Additional Papers

In addition to papers arguing the merits of positions taken on historical matters in the church, my yearlong journey with Church History required other assignments that required me to wrestle with church history. The first of these assignments required students to write a descriptive summary of their local ministry contexts where their churches continued to make additional church history. The second includes responses written as part of my midterm during my first semester that shows my thinking regarding the subject at hand. The third work presented below is a book review of Walter Rauschenbusch's seminal work *Christianity and the Social Crisis*. This review sheds light on my thought process as my theology evolved with the new knowledge of social justice beginnings in church history. Below, this chapter presents these works in the order in which they were written.

Descriptive Summary

My local context would benefit greatly from an examination of the component of music within worship during the reformation through the eyes of John Calvin and Martin Luther. This is because the reformation is tied to our identity as Baptists, music is a dominant part of our worship, and because only by examining the origins of our tradition can we evaluate the quality of ministry through music in my context.

Many people in our congregation do not understand the fact that our identity is tied to the Reformation in light of the fact that our denomination has been derived from the Protestantism that began due to the Reformation. In particular, most of the congregants in my context do not understand the impact of persons like Martin Luther and John Calvin. For example, the congregational style of singing that we utilize has its root in the theology and practice of Calvin.[1] The reason for limiting the discussion of music within worship to Luther's Lutheran tradition and Calvin's Reformed tradition is because along with Roman Catholicism they were the largest products of the Reformation. Having a firm grip on our identity would influence our worship practices and our witness in the world. This is because we cannot worship a God that we are seeking to know if we have no idea of who we are. This information could also inspire those in my congregation to be free to tailor the music to fit our clearer sense of identity.

Music is an extremely important part of our worship where through our worship we connect with God and with each other. Being in an African American church context, learning about the Reformation would help our context to better understand the European elements of our music given the fact that the Reformation was birthed in Europe. Our context needs to understand that the reformation is the movement through which the musical component of the Christian church, birthed through the protestant churches, was changed forever. An understanding of Calvin's impact is important because he emphasized congregational singing and removed the chorale and this helps to explain our congregational tradition to sing together sometimes without the help of a choir. At the same time, members need to know that Luther was a strong proponent of the chorale system and that we have elements of his tradition such as a strong tradition in hymnody. Our context needs to comprehend the fact that the reformation shifted the focus from the sacrament to evangelism and this explains the dominant theme of salvation in our music.

Learning about music in worship during the reformation will empower my congregation to make judgments concerning whether or not our current music in worship holds to these traditions. We can determine which elements of the changes to music during the reformation by Calvin and Luther should be maintained and if improvement is necessary in order to better reflect our current identity. This knowledge will empower our congregation to evaluate our music to see whether or not it is as evangelical as Luther intended or if it is as scriptural as Calvin intended. By analyzing our own music we can determine if we are holding to the paradigm established by Luther in which singing in worship is an enjoyable experience. A large amount of the music celebrated in many churches today is unscriptural and this produces mass confusion in the local church and in the larger church body. This will also help to safeguard our ministry from receiving or adopting music that does not reflect our understanding. By looking at the beginning of the ancestors to our denomination, our context should be able to assess whether or not according to our judgment that we have improved worship practices in a similar manner in which the leaders of the Reformation were able to improve the church.

Historical

Midterm Responses

Perpetua

Vibia Perpetua was a noblewoman who was martyred with her slave Felicity and others at Carthage in 203. Her martyrdom came as the result of a break out in persecution of Christians under the emperor Septimius Severus who ordered the persecution and attack against new converts as a means to discourage further conversions. This effort was the first part of four major waves of persecution which hand the intent of instilling greater loyalty among people in the Roman Empire (WCM pg 109). For Perpetua to come from a well-to-do family and join the Christian community was to subvert the authority of her father and to challenge the authority of Roman society by extension (WCM pg. 83). Perpetua was part of a larger movement of Christian believers who did not recant their professions of faith under the threat of martyrdom but instead viewed martyrdom as a validation of their faith. While awaiting execution she recorded a series of prophetic visions that were circulated after her death. In the end, when the beast did not kill her, she guided the blade of her executioner into her throat even as the gladiator's hand trembled and this demonstrated her courage, faith and state of mind that it was an honor for her to suffer for the faith. Not even the fear of leaving her nursing son behind could dissuade her from turning her back to the faith. One can suspect that her courage in the pattern of other martyrs before her only strengthened the commitment of other believers and attracted others to the Christian movement (WCM pg. 82). Perpetua is important because she is a face of the committed female believers who did not yield under persecution. She is also important because like others known for the same sort of courage, she served as a cultural witness to the character and courage of Christian believers who while a threat to the empire operated with integrity. Along with others, Perpetua provided "a point of self-definition for North African Christians" (WCM pg. 140). Perpetua was a contributor to Christianity getting its shape in North Africa.

Donatists

The Donatists were one of two parties that emerged as the result of a schism in 315 "over the status of clergy who were suspected of having collaborated with imperial authorities during the persecution" of Diocletian that began in 303 (WCM pg. 156, 167). These questionable clergy were also referred to as "fallen." The Catholics were the other side of this schisms and the controversy between the two groups over treatment of those labeled as "fallen" continued from the fourth through the six centuries where each party considered itself to be the true church. The Donatists considered itself to be the pure church on the basis of martyrdom. Although the Christian religion had acquired imperial support through Constantine, the Donatists out of North Africa were not willing to let the past go in part because their memories of martyrdom had fostered a unique sense of Christian identity. To the Donatists, martyrdom was an honorable thing and martyrs were able to intercede for living Christians after death. The Donatists refused to forget the transgressions of Christians who in the eyes of the Donatists had become "traditors" or traitors by turning over scriptures or liturgical books which in those days was considered on par with making offerings to the Roman gods. In the view of Donatists, any involvement on the part of traitors in the ordination or administering of sacraments made them invalid. With regard to ordination, if a person to be ordained was a traitor or was ordained by a traitor that meant that their ordination was invalid and that leader could have not received the Holy Spirit through the laying on of hands. Eventually the Donatists were suppressed for disturbing the peace at the order of Constantine and in the end their properties were taken and their leaders were arrested and sent into exile. This was the first time where a Christian government persecuted a Christian party because of a lack of unity in the religion. As a result, many Donatists were exiled and killed. The Donatists were important because they were the first Christians to be persecuted by other Christians. They were also important because of their emphasis on the connection between faithfulness and martyrdom and in counting the cost of being a Christian. They are further important to history in part because in their discontent with the Catholics they provided fertile ground in North Africa for the spread of Islam.

Ignatius of Antioch, *Letter to the Magnesians*

Ignatius, also called Theophorus, was the bishop of Antioch who wrote letters to churches while being transported on his way to Rome to be martyred during the rule of the Roman emperor Trajan (98-117). The rule of Trajan was a time where Christianity was illegal and people like Pliny the Younger took action to stop the spread of Christianity for the good of the empire. At the beginning of the second century the persecution of Christians became official policy. As a person about to be martyred and since he was sought out by the Magnesians his words would have great influence and so Ignatius used his platform to speak freely. Ignatius was part of the Christian leadership that helped the church in its search for identity with regards to leadership structure by endorsing a monarchial system of leadership that utilized bishops, presbyters and elders.

Ignatius at the beginning of the second century used the term catholic to describe the sense of connectedness that the bishops succeeding the original apostles had with them. This sense of connectedness was important in the context of Ignatius' argument for the preservation of unity partly based on the premise that the church of Magnesia should follow the bishops as the successors to the apostles and as extensions of God's authority. Specifically, this is why he called on the Magnesians to honor their bishop Damas, their presbyters Bassus and Apollonius and their deacon Zotion.

During his lifetime, there were those who claimed to be of the Christian movement who had alternative views on apostolic teaching and different interpretations of texts and traditions that were familiar to Ignatius among others, and this included Marcion (WCM pg. 72). This explains why Ignatius argued for the Magnesians to follow apostolic tradition in article XIII and why he connected their leadership with the leadership of Christ and the apostles. Tensions had arisen between the prophets and bishops in Asia Minor in the beginning of the second century. It is therefore sensible for Ignatius to exhort the Magnesians to be unified in their harmony with God and to love one another. He wrote during a time of persecution where he himself was being led away for execution. He wrote during a time where Christians were suspicious to the Roman authorities. It is in this context in which Ignatius cautions the Magnesians to be good examples and lessons of immorality in article VI.

Ignatius wrote his letters during a time in which the Docetists, people that believed that Jesus did not have a real human body but that his body was just a phantasm, were gaining a foothold with their teachings. It is in this context that Ignatius uses his Letter to the Magnesians to argue against vain doctrine and false teaching that does not affirm the reality of the birth, passion and resurrection of Jesus Christ. Since there were those who argued against Jesus' humanity, Ignatius implies that the birth and passion specifically refute this false teaching. Ignatius also believed that those who accepted this heretical view of Jesus' humanity were minimizing his impending suffering (WCM pg. 72). It is logical then that he argues in his Letter to the Magnesians that suffering is a symptom of true discipleship because suffering for the faith should not be diminished.

In Ignatius' context, the people and memories served as a stronger basis for the connection among them than some doctrinal statement or formulation. As a result, it is understandable that Ignatius would take time to remind the Magnesians of their connection to other Christians such as himself, the Ephesians from Smyrna and other churches. Everything else that he wrote in this missive can be best understood perhaps as the final wishes or will of a bishop for the church of Magnesia that reached out to him. In other words, in this the last time that he would likely be able to communicate with them Ignatius reminds them to be unified with God, leadership and each other. He further reminds the Magnesians to remember others in prayer, to live Christian lives, to remember that they are loved, and for them to cling to their faith.

Justin Martyr, *Second Apology*

Justin (d. ca. 165), a catholic author, was emerged in a context in which catholic apologists came forth to refute the heresies of Gnostics with scripture, apostolic tradition and reason and also by often using the same intellectual sources as the Gnostics. However, in the context of persecution and difficulties for Christians apologists focused on arguing that Christianity was not a threat to the empire. In other words, Justin "wrote to explain and justify the Christian faith in the context of Greco-Roman pagan culture" (RWC pg. 37). Justin came to Rome around 135 during a time where there was no apparent episcopal structure in the Christian church. Justin in his work First Apology chronicled church meetings in which the eucharist was given. Apparently during this time the "president of the brethren" would give thanks for the bread and the wine and then the deacons distributed food and took it to absent members. These meetings were most likely held in house churches that operated sans the authority of a bishop.

During Justin's time, many were suspicious of Christianity and believed the claims of some that Christians were godless and impious. To this Justin responds in Second Apology that Christians are largely misunderstood by people such as Crescens because of ignorance. This environment of suspicion explains why Justin wrote that he expected to be plotted against as other Christians were. It is in the context of the suspicions of the Romans and resulting persecutions of Christians that Justin sought to affirm the moral superiority of Christian character for the purpose of establishing that Christians were not a threat to the empire and this includes honesty. This explains why in his Second Apology he recounts the story of the wife who is turned over to authorities by her immoral husband because she did not want to share in his evils and presented him with a bill of divorce. In this narrative it is not the wife who is the threat to the decency and good order of society but rather her unbelieving husband who conducted himself without restraint and who directed his destructive efforts toward Ptolemaeus who indoctrinated his wife into Christianity. Justin recalled that Ptolemaeus true to Christian form did not buckle under the pressure but remained honest in spite of suffering for the faith. Justin's inclusion of Lucius, who gave thanks due to his impending martyrdom after speaking truth to the powerful Urbicus, and a third Christian further support Justin's argument with regard to the integrity of Christians. He points to their character and courage in the face of death as not reflecting the disposition of one who would have been living in wickedness and pleasure.

It would make more sense that the Christian movement was not a threat given the fact that there existed no concrete hierarchal system of authority. In other words, by highlighting the limitations of the movement to house churches Justin was reassuring the Roman authorities that there was not sufficient manpower or organization to mount some type of rebellion. Due to the suspicions surrounding Christians, it is logical that Justin would seek to divert the blame for false teachings and calamity in the world away from Christians to demons that are the byproduct of fallen angels with women. In this environment Justin sought to not only defend Christianity from false charges but also sought to emphasize the good that Christianity brought to society. To support this, Justin referenced how Christians were able to cast out demons after other measures had failed. Furthermore, another part of Justin's argument was centered on the premise that the existence of Christians on the earth was the only thing that was keeping God from destroying it.

Justin came forth into a highly philosophical environment. As a result, he and other catholic apologists made an effort to frame the Christian faith within the context of Hellenistic philosophy. Eventually the catholic party understood that it needed to essentially frame the gospel within a context that the Hellenistic philosophical society could readily understand. In order to defend the gospel and the Christian movement in this Hellenistic context, Justin in Second Apology wrote to the imperial senate to reassure its members that "Christian teaching embodied the best of Hellenistic philosophical traditions" (WCM pg.

120). Justin was especially equipped for this task to which he committed himself because he was a converted student of Greek philosophy. Such facts help explain Justin's numerous references to philosophy including Stoicism, Socrates, Plato and Xenophon. Since Justin lived in Rome in a pagan culture, he sought to equate Jesus, the head of the Christian movement, with the Logos which was familiar to his philosophical context. Justin argued that the premise of the logos within philosophy was correct but incomplete in that Jesus was the whole Logos who was used to create the world. Justin paints Jesus as the fulfillment or completion of the Logos idea. The climate of persecutions and distrust explain why Justin sought to connect philosophy with the gospel potentially under the premise that if we all believe in the concept of the logos then there is no true conflict in the teaching of the gospel and of philosophy. Justin also succeeded in connecting reason with suffering as he referenced the Stoics who suffered for reason's sake.

What should your local church leaders know about the first few centuries of the Christian church?

Local church leaders within my context should know that the first few centuries of the Christian church were all about establishing its identity. Included in this struggle were the dual goals to establish both what a Christian was and what a Christian believed. In an effort to inform local church leadership about this effort to establish identity, these leaders should be taught about the development of leadership, of the canon, and the importance of cultural witness.

Leaders from my local church context should know that during the first few centuries of the Christian church, the church developed its principles of how the church should be led and by whom. A senior pastor and a board of deacons comprise the spiritual leadership of my local church while the common structure in the early church included a bishop, deacons and presbyters. Understanding the differences in structure would help deacons for instance to see that they have to do the job of the traditional presbyter and deacon while the pastor operates as a bishop. Persons became leaders in the early centuries of the church principally through the process called apostolic succession where beginning with the disciples the followers of the church leadership would become the next generation of church leadership after being conferred by prayer and by the laying on of hands. Those who hold office in my local church need to know about these details because churches struggle today to appoint new leaders especially to the pastoral office in part because there is no model of succession and so this would help my local context to better plan for the future. An organized and planned succession for the pastoral office would reduce competition and confusion while providing for a smooth transition of leadership down the road. Also, with regard to leadership, our leaders should be informed of the fact that more levels of leadership were established in the church largely at the prompting of existing church leaders because of a need. This is important because leaders, even in my context, need periodic reminders of the fact that being called to leadership is a call to address the needs of the people and that these positions do not exist for the purpose of leaders being self-serving. The establishment of leadership was important because there were forces seeking to define the church from without such as cultural pressures and so current leaders would benefit from such information because it would remind them that they have a responsibility to prevent the corruption of our society from penetrating the walls of the church. The works of several scholars contributed to the church's understanding as to how the church should be structured in order to provide for sound leadership and a stable church. Leadership in my local context should become familiar with the names and ideas of some of these leaders such as Ignatius of Antioch, Clement of Rome and Hippolytus of Rome. This is due to the fact that being familiar with the aforementioned persons and their ideas would provide credibility for them because then they would be able to explain in part why leadership is structured the way it is in our local context. At the same time, being familiar with the traditional functions of church leaders from the first few centuries (i.e. presbyters advising the bishop) of the Christian church would help our leaders to be better informed about what is expected from them. Local church leadership should know about the leadership of the early church in part because leadership succession and ministerial integrity are still issues in the church today and it would be beneficial for local church leaders to gauge if they could have served as leaders in the early Christian church. At the same time, many churches are using charisma as the chief critique in appointing leaders but ministerial integrity should be more paramount than it is. The character traits put forth by works such as the Didache (i.e. meekness, not lovers of money, truthful, etc.) should be applicable to modern church leadership. By understanding the qualifications for leaders in the early church, it will help local church leaders to engage in self-examination for the purpose of determining if these leaders would have been considered for leadership roles in the early church as the result of their ethics.

After establishing a methodology for leadership and appointing leaders, the church of the first few centuries moved to identify itself based on the development of a canon for the purpose of having a text that guided the church and reflected an understanding of who the church was. Canon means a standard, rule or measuring rod. The canonization process needs to be defined for local church leaders because many of them have never heard of the process or have any understanding of how early Christians created the canon. Much of the leadership operates with blinders as far as being completely unaware as to how the Bible came into existence. One of the catalysts for the development of the canon was the development of canons of groups whose teachings were considered to be far from those the majority party considered to be true such as the Marcionites (WCM pg. 72). The Marcionites were followers of Marcion (d. ca. 155) who developed a canon of his own in which due to his beliefs in the existence of two Gods, the evil God of the Old Testament and the good God of Jesus, his canon consisted of the writings of Paul while rejecting the Old Testament. Leadership should be aware of the divergent views of the early church and how groups were divided on the basis of beliefs. If local church leaders knew this history, they could help ensure that the church does not get bogged down by fruitless debates about minute details by sharing with the congregation that the disputes so prevalent in our church are of little importance compared to the debates surrounding the nature(s) of Christ. Leadership should be informed of the process of canonization that consisted of four independent criteria: is the writing in the norm or used in worship, does the writing reflect the mind of the apostles and how, is the writing universal or common for the church, and lastly does the writing grow out of the understanding of self, worship and practices. The development of the canon was a process that used the previously mentioned criterion. An understanding of the canonization of scripture would be very useful for local church leadership so that it would understand what the Bible is and what the Bible is not. As a result of understanding this process our leaders could further understand and explain to the laity why some of the books were not included in the canon instead of clinging to an ignorant explanation of "inspiration" for the process. By exposing the biases against particular books church leadership would be able to understand that there are extra-biblical resources that can be used to provide greater context to the diversity of beliefs during the first few centuries of the Christian church. The leaders in my local context primarily would also be able to provide context for those that follow them as to why Christians follow the Bible and mostly reject other writings. Our leaders should also know about some of the key persons in the development of the canon which would become the Bible. These leaders included Athanasius, whose list of the current twenty seven books of the New Testament were accepted by the senate of Rome in 367, and about Augustine of Hippo who provided a list of a canon including the Old and New Testaments and some apocryphal books in 397. Leaders should also be aware that these books were being used prior to their canonization. Ultimately in the fifth century a canon was agreed upon and created as opposed to simply acknowledged. This would be important for leadership to know in order to not only understand how the Bible came into existence but also to equip them to share this truth with others.

Thirdly, the leaders in my local church context need to know about the cultural witness provided by Christians during the first few centuries that helped define what it meant to be a Christian. In this postmodern world where people often question whether or not religion brings anything good to society, Christians and leaders in particular need to know that the first few centuries of Christianity featured the ministry of well regarded apologists who defended the faith. One of the reasons that this is necessary is that the apologists of that era attempted to defend the faith against non-Christians and shared their faith in the midst of a society that did not want it or understand it. Many would argue that this attitude toward Christianity in particular is still prevalent today and so it would give our leaders an opportunity to study the approaches taken by these gifted apologists in order to know how to defend the faith in our context. For example, it would help our leaders to know about Justin, a catholic apologist, who defended Christianity to the Roman emperor and senate and explained that Christianity was not a threat. He also tried to show how Christianity fit in the Greco-Roman philosophical context. In this case, Justin argued that Christianity could be assimilated within the Roman culture. It would help current church leaders to appreciate the fact that we do not have to argue in this country to assure the powers that be that we should be able to coexist with unbelievers. Our leaders could also learn how to build arguments by studying the works of the apologists and then use those skills to argue against social ills and to argue that Christianity should pose a threat to unjust systems and circumstance. Another well known figure in the apologist movement was Tertullian who wrote for the purpose of communicating to Christian women how they should look. He argued that Christian women should not dress like the Gentile women and in doing so they would stand out and provide a counter-cultural witness. In contradistinction to Justin, Tertullian sought for lines to be drawn in the sand. Learning about Tertullian would help leaders in my context to encourage all of our members to be counter-cultural when and where necessary. Leaders could use this as a historical authority for arguing that there should be a difference in how the world sees Christians. In addition to the contributions in the area of cultural witness from apologists, there were also contributions in the form of martyrs. Our leaders should understand that during the first few centuries of the Christian church that believers were filled with courage and were made to suffer and die due to the persecution of the Roman emperor. Many times Christians were killed because they refused to worship or make offerings to Roman gods as the result of their Christian faith. Justin in his Second Apology told the story of how a husband told the authorities that his wife was a Christian as retribution for attempting to divorce him and she was likely martyred. This was a time of great danger and suffering for Christian believers. Leaders should be aware of the suffering of the believers that came before us in order to better appreciate the freedom with which we worship without having to worry about being martyred for the faith at least in our context. Also, leaders should know about the martyrs of North Africa and in particular Perpetua and Felicity so that they can relay the powerful and positive examples of early Christian women who were courageous in the face of martyrdom. Not only this, but leaders need to be able to communicate to our mostly African American congregation how North Africa produced some of the greatest minds and most courageous and faithful martyrs in all of the early centuries of Christianity. Our leaders should be aware of the pervasive faithfulness of the North African believers which lead them to greet each other and say "may you receive your crown" in order to convey their commitment so as to motivate the congregation to be more committed to the Lord they profess. To escape martyrdom, some Christians cooperated with the authorities and as a result some Christians, in particular the Donatists, refused to accept these "fallen" back into the fold. Our leaders need to know about this so that they will not hold other believers to such a high standard that it prevents their restoration according to the scriptures (Galatians 6:1).

This search for identity eventually continues in the next few centuries of the Christian church beginning with the collision of this search of identity with the first Christian Roman emperor in Constantine which would lead to the council at Nicea ending with a clear declarative statement to answer the question for Christians as to "who we are." This is all important for leadership to understand because the struggle for Christian identity almost two thousand years later is still not over.

Historical   71

Review - *Christianity and the Social Crisis*. By Walter Rauschenbusch.

Walter Rauschenbusch's book *Christianity and the Social Crisis* was originally written in 1907. It is the preeminent work on the topic of the social gospel and it provided the most aggressive definition of the social gospel to date even though it was written over a century ago. It contributes to the conversation by raising the problem if Christianity's inability to solve the social ills of his day and it is valuable because it brought to the forefront issues that are still prevalent in today's context. It contributes a call to arms, so to speak, for Christians to get to work and follow in Jesus' footsteps in caring for the whole person instead of just the spiritual.

The thesis of this work is that in response to the social and industrial change of society, those equipped by the gospel should wake up and act in the best interests of those affected and in doing so they truly live up to the title of Christian for the good of society as a whole. He supported his argument by claiming that the foundation on which Christianity was built supported the idea of social revolution, that Jesus and his first followers were engaged with the holistic needs of persons, and that in spite of past failures it was not too late for Christianity to act in congruence with the best designs of its namesake Jesus Christ. This thesis is extremely important for the discipline of practicing the social gospel because it teaches the Christian not to live his or her life in a vacuum but to see how others are affected and follow Jesus' example.

Rauschenbusch argued at the beginning of the book that the foundation for social impetus is found first in the ministries of the prophets and does this as means to show that social concern is as foundational to the Christian faith as the prophets. He then transitioned to discuss the social conscience of Jesus before addressing those first Christians and their attitude toward the social needs of the people. Rauschenbusch went on to articulate the problem of the Christian faith being its past failure to live up to its potential in aiding the process of social reconstruction. He then undergirds his argument by appealing to the self-serving interests of the church noting that the church would eventually be affected by these social ills because it is a sampling of the larger society. Lastly Rauschenbusch provided an answer to the question of "where do we go from here?" and called on the church to go forward in addressing the present social crisis brought on by the industrial revolution while intimating that the church should learn from the past. He did an excellent job in structuring this work, appealing to common sense and using scripture and other publications like books and journals and references to legends to support his thesis.

This work by Rauschenbusch possesses several strengths such as its structure, its clear arguments, and it was very effective in making the case as to why concern about social ills lies in the very heart of being a Christian. Some weaknesses include his perceived devaluing of individual spiritual change, especially its importance for ministry, and the fact he seemed to be overly idealistic about the capacity of Christianity to fix these social problems. The book was easy to read and follow and this was helped by the thorough table of contents which included summaries of each chapter. The index is also helpful to the reader as it deals with ideas and not simply key words. The audience that suits this text includes seminary students and others who have an understanding of the principle that in Paul's theology faith and works are two sides to the same coin. At the same time, it may find a home in all sorts of libraries as a reference work for historical Christian thought and even in the libraries of churches so that the members no longer remain content to sit in the comfort of the four walls of the church while the community in which the church sits is dying. Everyone, including those in need, can learn something from this text about what it means to be Christian beyond some salvific encounter with God.

Historical

Independent Study

The last of my works that I desire to put forth within the category of Church History is the result of an independent study course with the guidance of Professor of New Testament and Greek, Boykin Sanders, Ph.D. The memory as to how we arrived at the subject for this writing escapes me. I do remember, however, that part of the reason for focusing on this particular subject of "Wealth and Poverty in New Testament Times" related to the doctrines of prosperity and the plight of the modern poor. Studying the economic landscape of those who lived during New Testament times provides the necessary context to properly interpret the texts that spoke of money, but it also provides fodder for conversation with regard to the relationship between wealth or poverty and spirituality. The entire paper written during my final year of seminary lies below.

Wealth and Poverty in New Testament Times: A Correlation of Social Position and Beliefs Concerning Wealth and Poverty

Introduction

The aim of this composition is to present my findings with regard to how arguably the most important sects of Judaism viewed wealth and poverty in the context of New Testament times in light of these sects' social standing. This research is relevant to today's context for a variety of reasons. These reasons include the present economic turmoil in this country in particular which has arguably been exacerbated by the recklessness of the wealthy seeking to protect or grow their wealth with callous disregard for the poor among us and how their actions have further displaced many in their pursuit of the American dream. Those who praise capitalism when it works for them while at the same time seeking to limit or eliminate assistance for the poorest among us show that there is a natural correlation between one's social position how one sees wealth and poverty especially through one's hermeneutical lens of theology.

An additional reason in favor of the relevance of this research to the present is the extent to which the church has moved from a sense of community and aiding the poor to preaching a message of prosperity and promoting the wealth of the clergy who preach such a "gospel." I disagree with the premise of prosperity theology that all Christians can live in material abundance simply through the exercise of faith.[2] It is easy to accept and promote the idea of wealth being symptomatic of one being in right standing with God when those who preach this message are wealthy or become the beneficiaries of a self-fulfilling prophecy of wealth after using the emotions and hopes of the poor to numb them for fleecing. In contradistinction to this theology of prosperity, my theology accounts for the fact that the social position of persons depends on some of the factors that contributed to the material success or deficiency of these groups including politics and power. I cannot in good conscience accept a theology that somehow blames the poor for their social status and that credits the laziness or faithlessness of the poor for their economic condition. This is not consistent with the character of the God whom I serve. My theology is such that I do not believe that God is satisfied with a salvation that is only spiritual in nature but rather I hold that God desires for humanity to be whole in every aspect. This means that I do not believe that God is pleased with the seemingly never-ending expansion of the chasm between the rich and the poor.

The scope of this examination is limited to the Essenes, the Zealots, the Sadducees and the Pharisees. It covers not only what could be found in reference to their beliefs but also presents findings related to the social position of the members of these groups so as to connect the dots between doctrine or theology and social status. Put another way, this paper seeks to correlate the beliefs of these groups concerning wealth and poverty with any wealth or poverty that these groups experienced firsthand. "In antiquity political power and social station led to the acquisition and retention of wealth" and so it makes sense that there is a general correlation between the political status of these groups and their economic social condition.[3] While there exist primary sources for half of these groups (the Pharisees and Essenes) that can serve to help interested parties to encounter such relevant information, this paper is largely supported by resources that discuss the pertinent information from primary sources. For each sect, I will provide a brief history on each group before discussing the social status of these groups prior to lastly presenting my findings concerning the attitudes toward wealth and. At the conclusion of each section, I will reflect on what I have discovered and discuss whether or not my personal theology would have permitted me to align myself with any of these groups on the basis of their views alone. In other words, my own theology will serve as a hermeneutical lens through which I interpret the usefulness or applicability of the particular sect's views to my context.

The Essenes

Knowledge of the sect of the Essenes largely depends upon the primary source of the Dead Sea Scrolls discovered at Qumran in 1947 these scrolls were produced by a group of Essenes.[4] It is possible that this community was formed around 150 B.C.E "during the early Maccabean period.[5] It is possible that this sect came into existence as the result of a schism where priests "who felt drawn to a higher religious ideal" left the Sadducees and joined with the Assidæans in what came to be known as the Party of the Covenant.[6] According to another source, the members of the Essenes withdrew from the Jewish community because they feared a contamination of sorts through contact with persons who did not hold themselves to the same standards and who followed laws different from those of the Essenes.[7] Contextually speaking, the Essenes were among the group of ascetic communities who had a pervasive distrust of the material world.[8] Based upon this history and formation, one could expect them to desire to distinguish themselves from their contemporaries.

Upon investigation, it is apparent that the Essenes self-identified as the "community of the poor" in some of the primary sources of the Dead Sea Scrolls where poverty in this context referred to both spiritual and economic forms of lack.[9] Even the humble graves in which the remains of Essenes were found give credence to the notion that these people had a "spirit of poverty."[10] However, other sources cast doubt on the extent of their economic poverty. For example, the Essenes were not impoverished according to Philo's portrayal but used their common resources to provide sufficient food and other necessities for the entire community.[11] Josephus also remarked that there was no outward evidence of poverty or excessive wealth.[12] It is interesting that these of the Essenes did not pull together due to some sense of limited resourcefulness in an effort to pool their resources but bonded over ideals of piety. This was a sect free of economic ego as evidenced by the fact that "there were no distinctions amongst them such as rich and poor" as well as the fact that they had no need for a hierarchical system "because they had all things common."[13] These pious persons chose to need each other and therefore relied on one another. In this system, the Essenes provide an effective model for holistic ministry.

There is a strong correlation between the economic condition of the Essenes and their beliefs about wealth and poverty. It is no surprise based on their self-identification that the Essenes regarded poverty as a virtue as evidenced by their arrival at such a "moneyless" state by choice rather than due to some lack of good fortune according to Philo's praise.[14] Put another way, poverty was a strict ideal for the Essenes and so it is not surprising that, at least according to some, the Essenes held contempt for money and wealth.[15] Both Philo and Josephus in their writings refer to the spirit of community with which they shared their property but Josephus also mentioned that the Essenes were "despisers of riches."[16] Philo spoke of their "freedom from the desire for money" which shows that selfish and greedy individuals did not comprise the large part of this community.[17] It therefore seems that the Essenes only viewed wealth as a means by which to provide the necessities of the community and not as a means to elevate the importance or social station of a prosperous few.

These ideals were engraved onto the hearts of adherents from the beginning. In order to become part of this group, interested individuals would have to endure a two-year initiation and upon meeting approval the admitted would then need to "donate all of his possessions to the community fund."[18] Evidence suggests that this was not an attempt to control every individual's possession but reflected a spirit of self-denial that elevated the needs of the community of those of the individual. This practice was practical in the sense that the Essenes shared this common fund "from which the wants of the whole community alike were supplied."[19] Not only did the Essenes turn inward to their own people in order to assist but they along with other "Pharisaic fellowships" made it their duty to assist the poor who were not a part of their community.[20] They recognized the community of humankind and so were charitable to others and so "meek and lowly in spirit, and were so much beloved by those who belonged to other sects" that some among the sects discussed in this paper "lavished praise upon them."[21]

The Essenes were encouraged to help the poor as a means of conforming to the nature of God.[22] Proof of this can be deduced from information from within their hymns contained in the Dead Sea Scrolls which consistently elevated the importance of righteousness over wealth.[23] This seems to be consistent with a theology where God assists those who are poor and they believed God was on the side of the poor – their side.[24] They also believed that they should not seek after "economic improvement" because they would rely on God to improve their economic condition.[25] It should be noted that their feelings regarding sharing resources were likely related to their beliefs that the "apocalypse of the end of time" was coming soon.[26] This explains why the "Essenes forbade laying up of treasures upon earth" and expected persons to joining them to sell their possessions and "divide it among the poor brethren."[27] It seems as if they were more interested in coming together and conforming to the image of God while awaiting God's move where the last become first.[28]

The Essenes were correct in believing that the body of the righteous should come together and contribute to a common fund in order to assist the poor. For I also believe that God is on the side of the poor and this should move the church to consider if it truly reflects the nature of God when it ignores the plight of the poor. Furthermore, I can agree with the premise that God improves persons' economic conditions with the caveat that each of us is empowered to do something and then empowered to help others along the way. While I subscribe to the idea of divine providence, I also believe that this does not obviate each individual of his or her responsibility to use his or her gifts and abilities to provide for that individual.

The Zealots

The sect of the Zealots is likely the sect that Josephus refers to as the "fourth philosophical sect" apart from the Pharisees, Sadducees and Essenes who were generally aligned with the doctrine of the Pharisees but expressed and embraced a refusal to call anyone other than God master.[29] In fact, the Zealots were originally a part of the Pharisees before departing as the result of a difference which could be summarized in the phrase "God, sole leader and lord."[30] Apparently the Zealots were so intent on preserving "Israel's absolute conformity to the Torah and its complete loyalty to Yahweh as its sovereign lord" that they were willing to even resort to violence against their Roman oppressors and those who refused to reject Roman rule.[31]

The Zealots came to the forefront at a time when conditions were ripe for rebellion. This was a time when due to an increase in poverty among the population, many persons were left with a disposition such that the only thing that many of these impoverished had left to lose was their lives.[32] These impoverished persons were among those who comprised the "dispossessed" following the death of Herod I and these dispossessed included "discharged soldiers, slaves and shepherds, who were disposed to rebellion."[33] As a result of such harsh conditions, it is not shocking that "many who joined the resistance were... desperately poor."[34] The ranks of the Zealots were bolstered by peasants who suffered economic turmoil as the result of poor crops or the inability to pay tax bills.[35] In fact, it is likely that the Zealots included "many of the poor and dispossessed: for the tribute would have borne more hardly on the poor than on those with better economic resources."[36] It does not seem logical that one would be among the poor yet still support the status quo that caused the economic condition of the poor to further deteriorate. Additional poverty due to "guerilla warfare" only exacerbated the resistance of the Zealots.[37]

At the same time, the Zealots possessed a "close sympathy for the poor and unprivileged, and a corresponding antipathy toward the rich Jews whose wealth and social position made them pro-Roman."[38] This sympathy likely swelled as they observed more poor individuals who were driven to poverty or further entrenched in poverty as a result of Roman oppression. In a sense they were not against poverty itself but against the oppression both by the Romans and the political and religious hierarchies which promoted poverty. A portion of this oppression was economic in nature as the people were forced to pay a tribute to Rome. At the time of revolt in A.D. 66 persons were "seriously behind in their payment of tribute" and it is likely that such debt exacerbated the economic struggle of the poor within the Jewish community.[39] They sought to overcome the resistance of the upper classes who did not want to engage in rebellion. To overcome this resistance they aligned themselves with the poor when, in an act of great social significance, Zealots raided the archives and burned the ledgers that recorded the debts of the masses.[40] This act, according to Josephus, "encouraged the poor to rise against the rich" as it drew a sharp distinction between those who suffered under the status quo and those who either became wealthy or at the least saw their wealth preserved or enlarged by the status quo.[41] For the Zealots, social location within the aristocracy made one a prime suspect of "collusion with the Romans" and as such this suspicion only heightened the tension and conflict between "the nobility and the common people.[42]

It is possible that the apostle James, who was executed, was "in sympathy with the Zealots, who were hostile to the Sadducean sacerdotal aristocracy for their pro-Roman policy."[43] This is logical because the Epistle of James "is characterized by its sympathy for the poor and its animus against the rich and influential."[44] Some have postulated that Jesus was a Zealot because of Jesus' affinity for the poor and unprivileged along with derogatory statements attributed to Jesus regarding wealth perhaps gained in an unrighteous manner or the difficulty of the rich in being acceptable to God.[45] It must not be seen as an accident that Jesus, according to the gospels of Mark and Luke, selected a zealot, Simon Peter, who would be first among the twelve and then arguably the chief apostle of the church.[46] This would be one who shared Jesus' view of the poor and righteous indignation concerning the abuse of the poor by the rich and members of the political and religious hierarchies.

With regard to the beliefs of the Zealots, I can agree that freedom is worth fighting for; but I must disagree with the premise of enacting violence against persons who do not share my ideals. Evil must be exposed not only in the social inequalities perpetuated by ineffective social structures but also must be exposed in the hearts of those who either explicitly support such systems or implicitly support them in their refusal to speak against them. As we are seeing in the present economical debate in the United States, it is easy to pit the poor against the rich especially when it seems like the rich are self-absorbed and therefore support the status quo. I agree the spirit of the Zealots in the sense that when the status quo continues to hurt those among us who need the most assistance something must be done in order to give a voice to those whose voices have been silenced all in the name of capitalism and the almighty dollar.

The Sadducees

The sect of the Sadducees appeared sometime in the second century B.C.E. after the Maccabean revolt.[47] However ascertaining information about the origin of this group is difficult at best because no primary sources of information or "self-testimony" exists in order to help others understand exactly how this sect came into existence.[48] It is possible that the Sadducees "evolved from the ancient priestly line of Zadok, dating back to the time of King David in 1000 B.C.E."[49] The Sadducees were part of the aristocracy which in general "is defined by its political and economic role in society."[50]

With regard to the social status of those who comprised this sect, many sources support the notion that the Sadducees were among the wealthy individuals of their time. To begin, the Sadducees were the principle members of the Sanhedrin which had some rich members. The priestly hierarchy and associates also comprised the membership of the Sadducees and these members were likely to benefit and obtain wealth from the temple tax.[51] Furthermore, evidence suggests that the Sadducees "derived from the wealthiest strata of Jerusalem."[52] According to one source the Pharisees were more popular with the common folk and therefore this left "to Sadducism only the wealthiest high-priestly families."[53] The possessions and customs of the Sadducees also testified to the extent of their wealth. For example, among other things the Sadducees possessed "large tracts of land exposed to slave depredations."[54] The Sadducees also enjoyed excessive luxury in that they ate from vessels of gold and silver.[55]

Furthermore, in support of the notion of a Saducean composition of wealth individuals, even Josephus reported that "only the wealthiest of the Jews belonged to the Sadducees" and this suggests that wealth was a distinguishing characteristic for Sadducees.[56] While Josephus referred to them as being "first in rank" it is possible that this distinction was based on their doctrine or excellence in "arguing with their teachers rather than on the basis of their social status.[57] Along these lines, it is possible that simply because their philosophy was more likely to be accepted among society's elite that this was not somehow a reflection on the wealth of the Sadducees.[58] I would argue however through the lens of political corruption in today's context that such philosophy while not revealing wealth for the Sadducees would engender them to the rich and thereby availing resources to the Sadducees to which they would not otherwise have access. What is sure, is that in their own context, the Sadducees were "a force to be reckoned with" in part because they had accumulated wealth.[59]

The Sadducees perhaps indulged in riches because they believed that there would be no resurrection and that this life was all there was. This attitude led them to enjoy their lives while mocking the Pharisees for holding out hope for better when, in their minds, nothing better would come.[60] As previously stated, no primary sources exist from which we can derive explicit beliefs concerning wealth and poverty so this paper must rely on the implicit. The Sadducees' attitudes and beliefs concerning wealth can be deduced therefore from the fact that according to Josephus the Sadducees had the "confidence of the wealthy alone but no following among the populace" to which I previously alluded.[61] The Sadducees aligned themselves with the Roman authority and so would likely not have objected to the poverty that resulted from Roman occupation and oppression. They retained their status as they "collaborated with the Roman rule."[62] Put another way, in contradistinction to the Zealots, the Sadducees "made a pact" with the Romans that would have likely secured their political and economically prosperous futures.[63] However, similarly to other blocs, the Sadducees were not perfectly uniform in their support of Rome even though it is likely that the Romans used groups like the Sadducees to "control provincial societies."[64] Therefore it seems logical that they would be in favor of persons gaining wealth and retaining wealth even if it meant supporting the Roman oppressors since as previously stated they were likely to benefit and become enriched from oppressive practices.

Overall, given the current state of my theology, I could not imagine being a part of the Saducean sect. Given the plight of my ancestors who suffered as slaves under the oppressive controls of persons who thought of them as less than human, I could not bring myself to support the oppressive Roman rule purely for the sake of self-preservation or in order to swell my own net worth. While I understand that the drive to be self-centered stemmed from an eschatology free from resurrection, it is inconsistent with my theology to enjoy my success in a vacuum while ignoring the suffering of others regardless of what waits for us beyond the grave.

The Pharisees

The Pharisees, similarly to the Sadducees, appeared shortly after the Maccabean revolt which took place in 167 B.C.E.[65] However, there appears to be no consensus concerning the nature of this sect. The Pharisees have been described by various authorities in several ways including "as a leading political group, an influential religious party, an academic group, and a lay movement seeking the priesthood."[66] In terms of political involvement, the Pharisees did not cooperate directly with the Roman authority but generally supported a position where they would seek to avoid confrontation with the authority.[67] The name of this group "was probably derived from perushim ("separate") to refer to those who struggled to set themselves apart from the defiling religious practices of the ruling powers."⁶⁸ In fact, both Essenic and Pharisaic movements "came into existence" in response to the "political and secular direction of the upper classes."⁶⁹ In this way it seems that wealth itself was not regarded as the enemy of Pharisaic ideals but rather it was the actions of the wealthy that insulted the zeal of these groups to practice the law with integrity. The "degree of their zeal and their consistency in the common aspirations of the citizens of the holy community" rather than the "peculiar content of their will" is that which distinguished the Pharisees from the general population. ⁷⁰ The Pharisees were mostly concerned with laws governing holiness and this passion "was sometimes carried to extremes (Matt. 23)."⁷¹ In other words, the extent to which they desired excellence in the holy community served as their defining characteristic that separated them from the rest of the populace during these times.

There seems to be some conflicting information concerning the exact class of the Pharisees. One source states that the Pharisees did not have "independent wealth and power" but depended upon the governing class.⁷² In this way, the Pharisees would only have access to wealth or the benefits of wealth by serving under those who governed and who possessed wealth themselves. But another source states that some Pharisees were part of the governing class and of the Sanhedrin.⁷³ It seems as though there was always some connection between political clout and wealth although it seems that wealth accompanied political strength rather than being the means by which people attained political clout. While the assumption has been that by and large the Pharisees were poor on the basis of both Josephus and the Talmud, not all Pharisees were poor.⁷⁴ Instead they were likely a part of the retainer class, a class below and utilized by the ruling class, which consisted of persons who were not wealthy and at the same time did not have vocations typical of those in the lower class.⁷⁵

As part of this retainer class, the Pharisees, who angled for power and position in politics, could not have been "peasants or urban craftsmen."⁷⁶ However, it is likely that the Pharisees collected tithes as a part of their role as retainers.⁷⁷ As a result, it is possible that the authority to collect tithes granted them the ability to accumulate wealth rather than the funds being used for their survival and the same for the poor. This reflects the spirit of today's church where many religious leaders use more of the church's treasury to simply survive to the extent that they have become rich. The retainer class covered a few of the poverty scale categories which suggests that it is difficult if not impossible to confine the population of the Pharisees to rigid classifications such as poor or wealthy. However, it is clear that they were not among the sixty-eight percent of the population of a typical large city in the Roman Empire who were at or below subsistence level.[78] The Pharisees, according to Josephus, did not live in excess but "lived meanly, and despised delicacies" which suggests that even if the Pharisees possessed wealth they were not in the business of flaunting their riches or indulging in the pleasures that wealth could procure.[79]

For the Pharisees, beliefs about wealth and poverty did not exist in vacuum but were a part of the larger picture of faith. For instance, the Pharisees believed in "another world" after death and this may have been the primary motivation for the Pharisees to abandon the pursuit of this world's "pleasures and material goods."[80] The Pharisaic abandonment of the pursuit of material success still was not mutually exclusive from their efforts to make the world a better place for humankind to live.[81] In other words, their belief in a utopian place beyond the grave did not somehow prevent them from expending their energy and resources to work toward a peaceful and harmonious society in this world. It is possible therefore that this ethic would lead them to assist their fellow men that were born equal to these the Pharisees. The Pharisees urged their people to replace the common morality which holds "What is mine is mine and what is yours is yours," with this unselfish principle: "What is mine is yours and what is yours is your own."[82]

Being zealous concerning the Law, one would expect that the Pharisees would have accepted what the Torah recorded specifically regarded the expectation of Jews concerning their treatment of the poor. For although Judaism rejected materialism this does not mean that in this belief system that poverty served as an ideal.⁸³ Instead the poor were described as miserable among other things and those who did not require assistance and had it to give were encouraged to give the tenth in order to help the poor with the understanding that no individual is able to access wealth from beyond the grave.⁸⁴ This spirit of charity has been adopted by persons in today's context, such as Warren Buffet and Bill Gates, who are lauded for their donations to charity in view of the fact that they possess more money than they could spend in several lifetimes. The Pharisees in their rigorous pursuit of following the Torah should have heeded the command for others not to take advantage of those who were poor or similarly disadvantaged.⁸⁵ One could likewise expect that those Pharisees fortunate to have their own harvest from fields or vineyards would allow the poor to glean from these resources.⁸⁶ The Pharisees followed Rabbinic teaching which instructed persons to give alms. Such instruction in part could have been derived from such entries in the Torah as Deuteronomy 15 which instructed Jews to be kind toward the poor even being charitable toward the poor among them with an open hand.⁸⁷ This kind of giving was "a special mark of Pharisaic piety" along with the extension of tithes according to Luke 18:12.⁸⁸ The Pharisees therefore would have viewed the poor as persons who they had a duty to assist. Evidence which supports the notion of obligatory assistance includes the existence of Pharisaic groups during those times which participated in a "distribution to the poor"⁸⁹

In addition to the Torah, the Gospels are also a source from which one can glean information about the beliefs of the Pharisees but these sources may not be the best or most impartial sources when examining the ethics and values of the Pharisees. The Gospel writers in many instances "gave an inadequate presentation and an incorrect picture of the real aims and aspirations of the Pharisees."⁹⁰ In other words, the writers of the Gospels misrepresented the ethics and goals of the Pharisees and Luke's portrayal of this group would be included in this word of caution. The Gospel of Luke in its sixteenth chapter and fourteenth verse famously depicted the Pharisees as being "lovers of money" but it is not fair to judge the Pharisees as such because they "did not accept that role."[91] The Gospel of Luke further presented the Pharisees as being uncaring about the poor.[92]

The singular aim of the Pharisees was to "fulfill the Law" and this, at least for them, left no room for pursuing practical goals that could result in changing the circumstances for some on earth including the least of these.[93] The Pharisees were so intent on fulfilling the letter of the Law and living according to the interpretations of the Law that they missed the spirit of the Law entirely. These zealous persons viewed the Torah as a means to an end (the righteousness of God) rather than as an imperative to assist their fellow human beings especially the poor.[94] Caution concerning the Gospel witnesses aside, according to Matthew chapter 6 reported that the Pharisees gave to the poor but did it to obtain prosperity from God by obeying God's command. This approach could have been validated in their eyes through the use of Deuteronomy 28:12-13 where wealth and plenty are signs of God's blessing.[95] They may also have interpreted Deuteronomy 8:18 as a statement reflecting some correlation between one's material wealth and their relationship with God. Therefore it seems likely that the Pharisees viewed wealth as a symptom of their approval from God and conversely this could have led them to consider the very poor to be cursed but yet still blessed through the alms the Pharisaic extension of God's grace.

While I applaud the zeal of the Pharisees my theology rejects the idea of assisting those who are less fortunate simply to be approved by God. In Christian terms, this seems to reflect a spirit of seeking justification by works rather than by faith. However I do subscribe to the idea that those who have the resources to help others have a duty to do so. Christians have the responsibility of representing God's character to all people and this includes mimicking God's concern for the holistic wellbeing of everyone. In support of these efforts, individuals of the church should give liberally and above the tenth if one can afford to do so. Lastly, wealth does not reflect one's standing with God but rather God sides with those who are less fortunate and those who are abandoned and cast aside.

Conclusion

As I have documented, in New Testament times there existed a strong correlation between a sect's social standing and their beliefs concerning wealth and poverty but not always in the paradigm of today's religious groups. Each of these sects had agreeable traits within their theologies of wealth and poverty but they each demonstrate the difficulty of achieving a perfect model for today's context. It is my hope that this paper has shed some light on this subject so that we can learn from the missteps of the past to arrive at a place in ministry that better reflects God's intent.

---

[1] McElrath, 153.
[2] Smith, 188-189.
[3] Saldarini, 23.
[4] Ehrman, 48.
[5] Ehrman, 50.
[6] Dupont-Sommer, 70.
[7] Ginsburg, 7-8.
[8] Weaver, 369.
[9] Pilgrim, 36.
[10] Dupont-Sommer, 7-8.
[11] Phillips, 120.
[12] Dupont-Sommer, 66.
[13] Ginsburg, 8.
[14] González, 13.
[15] Dupont-Sommer, 159.
[16] Dupont-Sommer, 65-66.
[17] Phillips, 119.
[18] Ehrman, 51.
[19] Ginsburg, 8.
[20] Pilgrim, 45.
[21] Ginsburg, 20.
[22] Murphy, 243.
[23] Murphy, 246.

[24] Murphy, 227.
[25] Murphy, 190.
[26] Ehrman, 50.
[27] Ginsburg, 23.
[28] C.f. Matthew 20:16.
[29] Brandon, 34.
[30] Wellhausen, 17.
[31] Brandon, 46.
[32] Hengel, 324.
[33] Hengel, 329.
[34] Pilgrim, 40.
[35] González, 50.
[36] Brandon, 56.
[37] Pilgrim, 40-41.
[38] Brandon, 325.
[39] Brandon, 49.
[40] Pilgrim, 41.
[41] Brandon, 132.
[42] Horsley, 175.
[43] Brandon, 169.
[44] Brandon, 169.
[45] C.f. Matthew 19, Luke 6:20, 16.
[46] Mark 3:18, Luke 6:15
[47] Miller and Miller, 206.
[48] Simmons, 66.
[49] Simmons, 68.
[50] Saldarini, 23.
[51] Pilgrim, 42.
[52] Finkelstein, *The Pharisees: The Sociological Background of Their Faith*, 80.
[53] Finkelstein, "The Pharisees: Their Origin and Their Philosophy," 191.
[54] Finkelstein, "The Pharisees: Their Origin and Their Philosophy," 222.
[55] Finkelstein, "The Pharisees: Their Origin and Their Philosophy," 189.
[56] Finkelstein, "The Pharisees: Their Origin and Their Philosophy," 189.
[57] Goodman, 142.

[58] Goodman, 142.
[59] Simmons, 70.
[60] Hatina, 64.
[61] Stemberger, 12.
[62] González, 49.
[63] Reinhartz, 232.
[64] Goodman, 145.
[65] Miller and Miller, 207.
[66] Hatina, 49.
[67] González, 49.
[68] Phipps, 19.
[69] Pilgrim, 39.
[70] Wellhausen, 15.
[71] Miller and Miller, 207.
[72] Saldarini, 106.
[73] Saldarini, 106.
[74] Finkelstein, *The Pharisees: The Sociological Background of Their Faith*, 186.
[75] Hatina, 53.
[76] Saldarini, 42.
[77] Saldarini, 296.
[78] Friesen, 20.
[79] Lauterbach, 151.
[80] Lauterbach, 151.
[81] C.f. Lauterbach, 152.
[82] Phipps, 22.
[83] Forta, 115.
[84] Forta, 115.
[85] C.f. Gowan, 341-342.
[86] C.f. Exodus 23:11, Leviticus 19:9-10.
[87] Deuteronomy 15:7.
[88] Pilgrim, 45.
[89] Pilgrim, 47.
[90] Lauterbach, 93.
[91] Stemberger, 31.
[92] Saldarini, 176.
[93] Wellhausen, 16-17.
[94] C.f. Wellhausen, 17.
[95] Levine, 127.

3

Practical

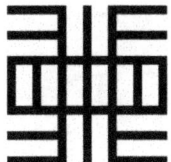

This chapter focuses on classes devoted to practical theology apart from preaching. One of such classes included the class of Church Administration where we discussed leadership and how to manage the business of the church. The assignment given in that class which I have chosen to include is an assignment called a "Problem Solution" paper. More will be stated about this paper below after devoting space to the works produced as the result of time spent immersed in ministry contexts and the work produced in a final reflective course entitled Senior Seminar.

One of the elements which separates the Master of Divinity curriculum from others is the extra emphasis and space allotted for students to put into practice the theory they learn by working in ministerial contexts with other trained practitioners. These courses belonged to a category of classes termed Field Education. As part of these courses, the curriculum required students to spend a minimum number of hours volunteering within social service and ministry contexts to get a better understanding of the intricacies of ministry in different contexts. These courses met monthly and served to remind students that ministry contexts did not simply include churches but extended to social services. In each case, students served under the supervision of responsible persons who provided written and verbal evaluations of the student's performance. Earl Bledsoe, D.Min., who served as director of field education, taught each of these classes, which spanned entire academic years.

Field Education I

The first of these courses, Field Education I, took place during my first year in seminary. This course required the completion of several assignments including a reflection on a church visit, a service verbatim, and a paper on Walter Rauschenbusch. The course also required 120 volunteer hours at a social service organization between November and April. Through a friend at my church, Rev. Tracey Cherry, I obtained an internship with the YWCA of Anne Arundel County where I participated with Mentoring, a domestic violence intervention program, and an after-school program called the Star Academy. In each of these I assisted where necessary and appropriate and garnered praise from those who led these programs. At the end of this first course, I completed a paper that included the lessons I learned during my experience. This paper follows.

The experience of volunteering my services at the social service agency, the Young Women's Christian Association (YWCA) of Annapolis and Anne Arundel County was an experience I will not forget. I was able to volunteer at a middle school for the Star Academy and at the local YWCA for both the Abuse Intervention Program (AIP) and the Mentoring Program. The YWCA has a clear mission of eliminating racism and empowering women in particular but its services also function to improve society. In my specific volunteering context, the mission was to empower young people of middle school age and to help them develop better academic and social skills but also meeting their holistic needs. Initially part of my responsibility was to sit in and contribute to the dialog between an AIP coordinator and the client who had been arrested for domestic violence. The YWCA ensured that the mission of this program was clear: to educate the abuser and thereby hopefully prevent a reoccurrence of this violent behavior for the good of the client, the abused and society. The individual missions of my particular contexts although stated before my experience began became clearer during my service.

From my experience I can state that the YWCA strove to fulfill its mission in each program. Each of the areas to which I was assigned had site leaders or facilitators who were entrusted with ensuring that the mission was fulfilled at each site. To this end, I can definitively say that the employees of the YWCA strove to meet their mission without exception. At the same time, these facilitators or leaders had the support of their upper management who ensured that these leaders were sufficiently equipped to meet the mission and the members of this upper management also conducted site visits to be sure that the hired leaders performed satisfactorily. Meeting the mission at the Star Academy was not an easy task because the students had at least four different site leaders during the school year and so they were forced to adjust to the personalities of these different leaders. The YWCA always strove to have dedicated and able faculty to lead all of the activities that I witnessed.

Overall, the YWCA fulfilled its promises to its clients, both the abuser and the students in need of assistance, through the programs to which I was assigned. In my experience with the AIP program, the particular client with whom I worked was able to understand his behavior after participating in the sessions and came to further understand how he could avoid future lapses in judgment and violent behavior toward his significant other. The program successfully led the client to take full responsibility for his actions and he was able to see that the problem stemmed from the dysfunctional relationship and from his past witnessing of violence between his parents.

The Mentoring Program kept its pledge to its clients by encouraging social interaction among the students, some of which were medicated. These students were referred to the YWCA by the county mental health department and the agency succeeded in getting these young people to open up about themselves. It also succeeded in getting these students to interact with other young people and adults using games and other activities geared toward self-discovery and self-esteem like the painting of self-portraits. The Mentoring Program always served dinner and usually a dessert and so it carried out its mission of ministering to these students in a holistic manner.

The Star Academy fulfilled its promises to clients for the most part by helping students with their homework and providing an opportunity for the students to engage with each other in recreational activities. Each day, from Tuesday through Thursday, provided a snack, homework time, a teaching element and recreation time and each of these things is outlined in the requirements by those who provide funding for the program. Over the course of my time in the Star Academy, I observed the development of the students but I'm sure that the inconsistency in leadership played a role in limiting the growth of these students at least academically during this time. There were two other volunteers who assisted along with myself and we were able to ensure that these programs made good on its guarantees to its clients.

The agency seemed to have sufficient funding to adequately staff the programs in which I volunteered. Per my discussions with leadership it was apparent that funding for the Mentoring Program and the Star Academy came from grants. On the other hand, it appeared that the funding for the Mentoring Program is secure. Attendance became an issue for the Star Academy attendance because the available amount of grant money is connected to the number of enrolled students. At the present time the leaders of the YWCA are looking to boost enrollment to ensure funding for next year. If the census fails to stay above the minimum, the Star Academy may not be at the site where I volunteered next year. With regard to AIP, due to a legal issue, the AIP Program is not able to use grant money and so they charge each client $40 per session which occurred once per week. If the client does not inform the leadership of the program of an impending absence that client still has to pay for the session that he or she missed.

Throughout the programs that I serviced, the demographics were very diverse. In the Mentoring Program, the agency's clients were diverse. There was a two to one ratio of boys to girls and there was the same ratio of white students to black students. For the most part, the ratio of staff to client matched the ideal ratio of one to one for a mentoring program. All of the students came from middle class families and as previously noted all of them are currently in middle school. The religion of these students was not apparent as none of them wore any religiously symbolic clothing or discussed their religion in the context of the mentoring sessions. In the AIP Program, the clients are also from a diverse set of backgrounds and this is no surprise given the fact that domestic violence crosses ethnic, economic and gender lines. The particular client with whom I interfaced was a white male in his early forties and he was firmly in the upper middle class. He shared that he made over six figures and so he had no problem paying the $40 fees for each session. In our discussions, nothing he said would imply that he ascribed to any particular religion. In our context, the ratio of staff to client including myself was two to one but usually the ratio would be about two staff to every twenty clients. At the same time, based on discussions with others there were also people in the program who were in the middle class and some also who were poor.

In the Star Academy, all of the clients were in the middle class and it seemed that most of them were Christians based on things they said and chants they repeated such as "I Am a C.H.R.I.S.T.I.A.N." As the census has shifted over the year the racial demographics of this clientele has also changed from having a majority of white students to having just about an equal number of white students to black students. The biggest disparity in demographics is with regard to gender where there are currently only four boys to eleven girls. Including me, the number of staff during my tenure fluctuated between three and six while the number of students fluctuated between fifteen and twenty-five.

All of the clients in each program were treated with dignity and respect by other volunteers and the YWCA staff. In the youth focused programs of Star Academy and the Mentoring Program, the students needed and received more patient instruction and tender loving care from the YWCA staff. No staff member ever became involved in physical contact with a client that was not playful in nature. In AIP, the client was treated like an adult and someone who deserved respect even though he made a mistake. In all of these programs the YWCA staff never adopted a judgmental attitude but sought to do what was in the best interest of their client and upholds the mission of the agency. Generally, the attitude of the agency's staff when the clients were not around did not differ from the positive attitude that was displayed in the presence of the client. The exceptions I observed occurred in the Star Academy where one particular staff member degraded one of the students privately in the audience of other staff and other students to whom she was close.

The YWCA provided ongoing services and training in each of the programs that I was involved. The Star Academy and Mentoring Program operate during the majority of the school year and offers its services throughout except in the event of school closure or if afternoon activities for schools in the county are cancelled. The AIP Program offers its services during the entire year and each client enrolls in the program for twenty-eight weeks to ensure rehabilitation through education and group sessions. Per my understanding, the YWCA does offer one time emergency help for some of its services but not for the services in which I volunteered my assistance. Based on this commitment to excellence and providing ongoing services along with the other things mentioned previously, if I were going to grade the agency and the staff a grade it would be an A-. The agency is extremely effective in making a difference it its clients lives and changing the path of some of them forever. In other words it is proficient and efficient in the services that it provided. My reason for giving the YWCA an A- is due to some issues with its staff and its inability at times to better market its services.

During my time of volunteer service, I learned a number of things that will help me in ministry and that will help to shape my mission and style of ministry. In general I learned that sometimes ministry will necessitate me going outside of my comfort zone in order to get things done. I also learned that in ministry one will come in contact with a diverse array of people from different backgrounds, some of which have great personal issues and may even be on medication. As a result, I understand that my style of ministry has to be conducive to multiple personalities and I need to exhibit patience, tender care, wisdom and understanding in order to be effective and not alienate the very ones to whom I am called to minister. Part of this is first understanding that people have not necessarily done anything to put themselves in the positions that they are in. This enables one to connect with people on a deeper level.

My time allowed me to see that ministry must inspire and encourage but also challenge the members of that particular ministry. It was also revealed to me that ministry needs to be holistic and as a result minister to the whole person but also that sometimes only fellowship is necessary. I was able to see that in ministry standards need to be set to set an expectation for what is acceptable and what is not. In the Mentoring Program sometimes a particular mentee's mentor did not come and so someone else had to substitute. This helped me to understand that in ministry people need to be in place to stand in the gap and substitute for others and the ministry should not rise or fall on any one person who is not named Jesus.

My style of ministry will be shaped by the lesson I learned from the YWCA in that having the right people in the right places makes all the difference. Part of my ministry's mission needs to be to empower people and trust people to operate in the areas of their particular gifts. One thing I attained because of my experience is that people generally have a level of respect for ministers but in the end more respect must be earned through upright living and living up to a godly standard. From the departure of some students from the Star Academy I ascertained that in ministry you cannot control who comes and who does not but just do what you can. I thank God for this opportunity to serve and all of the lessons about ministry that were exposed to me during my time of volunteering.

Practical

Field Education II

The second Field Education course took place during my second year of seminary. This particular year focused on immersive ministry within ministry contexts where students served under other clergy who possessed the Master of Divinity degree at a minimum. Part of completing this course included the completion of a Church internship verbatim and the compilation of a Church Polity and Planning Manual. As with the previous year's course, we needed to complete 120 hours of volunteer service at this context from November until April. With assistance from my pastor, I secured a mentor in Harold Knight, D.Min. who allowed me to intern with him over the course of that academic year. I assisted him at the New Shiloh Baptist Church in Dundalk, MD in various pastoral ways including providing advice to a ministry leader, assisting with baptism (providing the homily), and participating in Holy Communion. He also provided positive feedback about my job performance and we remain friends. As part of the course requirements, I completed a final assessment for this course and this assessment follows.

Words cannot completely encapsulate the gratitude that I have for the school of theology's requirement that we as students receive the practical instruction from field education. In transitioning from ministering to persons in a social service context to the church context I have found that the needs of those in the church that must be met mirror needs found in the social service context. These needs include the need to feel valued and I am grateful for the experience in both field education experiences that have shaped me into a better minister by making me more culturally aware of the milieus in which I minister. This year, I had the opportunity to minister at the New Shiloh Baptist Church in Baltimore, Maryland and my mentor was Dr. Harold L. Knight. This year's experience was particularly valuable for me because I have never had to minister, outside of preaching, to a congregation outside of my normative context. My home church has been that since I was ten years old and I do not believe I would have learned as much as I did had I been working in context that I have occupied for the past twenty years. That stated, this experienced provided an opportunity to get a glimpse of the pastoral ministry to which I feel a call and as the result of it I learned a great deal about God, about church, and about myself.

Being in relationship with a different church and having to provide ministry to that church in that context taught me some things about God while affirming other things that I previously knew or suspected about God. I learned that sometimes God will provide experiences that are designed to expose one's faith or trust and commitment to God. Sitting under a mentor that had previously graduated from the School of Theology, it helped me to see in general that God blessed those who have answered the call to ministry and been faithful in the pursuit of truth. Specifically, I saw that God had rewarded one who had been faithful to what he learned in seminary as opposed to those who seek seminary for credentials and who have failed to absorb all that seminary has to offer. It taught me the lesson that God can and sometimes will connect you with persons that have stood where you are standing so that they can help you navigate the journey.

At the same time, I learned that God is patient and empowering where God empowers persons to do the work that God has assigned them to do. I observed this through the effective ministry of my mentor but also through my ministerial effectiveness while assigned to do the work at this context. Lastly, it was reaffirmed to me how God can use anyone to do anything that God desires. It is humbling to me to know that God chose to trust me with preaching and teaching the word. This experience taught me how important it is to be myself and that God honors those who are authentic and do not attempt to masquerade under to personality of someone else. God is most glorified in our lives when we stay in our lanes and are authentic no matter what it costs us. In comparing this context to my home context, I was able to see that God likes diversity because between the two congregations God has chosen to use a diverse set of people. The people at the place of internship were different from the persons in my normative context. This church had far less youth and young adults but many more willing workers. The workers at the context of internship were no less called and equipped than those of my home church context. I learned that God will use circumstances to underscore the commonalities that exist among all of humanity.

As far as the church is concerned, I learned a number of things from this field educational experience. By comparing the practice of the Lord's Supper at in the educational context to that of my home church I was able to learn that that too many times in the church we rush things and go through the motions without soberly understanding why we as Christians do what we do. For example, through the solemn celebration of the Lord's Supper at the context of my internship I was able to see that the church needs to be more faithful in reverencing what God has done and the ordinances established to remember Christ's sacrifice. In addition to this I was able to ascertain the understanding that many problems that face different churches are universal such as faithfulness, giving, and normal issues that are found within any set of persons that are in relationship. I also learned that the relationship between pastor and leaders and pastor and members is very important in order to get everyone on the same page. This is because it takes a lot of trust on the part of the membership in order for the pastor to have the leeway to lead but that the giving of oneself to a congregation can be thoroughly rewarding for the pastor.

To that end, the majority of what I learned about the church is connected to being a pastor. For example, I came to understand that a pastor must have an understanding of not just the spiritual things of the church but also the business side of the church. At the same time, I came to see that when it comes to pastoring there is no substitute for authenticity and that church folk have no patience for persons who seek to fool others and God. There were a number of little things that I was able to see that go into being an effective pastor such as time management, diplomacy, being seen and heard, counseling, preaching, teaching, organization, and having integrity as the pastor represents the invisible presence of God. Also, the pastor needs to run a tight ship, be demanding when necessary, be resourceful and work to empower others while pleasing God. With regard to pastoring, I came to know alternate ways of baptizing, officiating communion, running a worship service and training ministerial staff through this experience. I also learned that sometimes things happen causing a pastor to have to change plans at the last minute but also that a pastor must never position the church as a higher priority than their family to the extent that their family is neglected in the name of ministry.

In the end, I also learned a good deal about myself including things about my personal views and theology, what I am able to do in ministry, and the areas in which I need to improve in order to pastor effectively. With regard to my theology, I learned that I believe in the responsibility of the kingdom of God to minister to the holistic needs of persons and I witnessed that in my experiential context. I was able to see that I do not believe that the influence of God and God's liberating power should be confined to the Sunday morning service(s) but should permeate everyone's existence according to the will of God. From a practical standpoint, I learned that coming into this experience I had a limited view of the pastoral ministry but now I am able to see much more of what being a pastor of a congregation requires not only of me but of my family. However, I was able to see that my ideas about minister were not that far out there after discussing theology and ministry with my mentor.

This experience taught me that I need to be honest about what is possible in ministry. I was able to learn that I can be instrumental in moving a church forward but that no church should be dependent upon me to make God proud. An aside to that is how this experienced helped remind me of the fact that while I need God, God does not need me. I learned through interfacing with strangers that I do not have much of a problem trusting or empowering people and this will serve me will in the pastoral context. I learned that given the correct context I will be able to take much of what I have learned from seminary and implement changes as necessary to the church who calls me to pastor. This is because, as I stated previously, my mentor is a graduate of the School of Theology and I can see the school's prints on some of the things that he does. Part of that includes making changes to the theologies observed in some of the creeds of the Baptist church such as the church covenant and how he goes about baptizing candidates for such. Field education has made me a better rounded minister by providing practical opportunities for experience in order to develop social skills critical for success in ministry that I did not previously possess.

In light of this good news, I also learned that there are some areas in which I must grow in order to be effective and it begins with personal devotional time apart from school assignments and even preaching assignments. I must find more time to take care of all of my business including God's business and the business of building a relationship with God. I have to be careful lest I become consumed with the work of God and go through the motions in my relationship with the God of the work. Also, I learned that I need to acquire more patience for dealing with persons whose personalities my not necessarily mesh with my own. I need to watch my body language and facial expressions not so I may be inauthentic but so that there is no contradiction between what I say and how it is perceived. In other words, I need to be careful so that my charisma is not overshadowed by outward expressions that may intimidate the people. I learned that as organized as I am, I need to be more organized but not necessarily completely rigid. In fact, I learned that I need to be more open and flexible in ministry.

As far as a growing edge, this experience helped me to become aware of the fact that sometimes I take people for granted and I cannot afford to do this in full-time ministry. On a sobering note, I was reminded that I am replaceable and so I should never get to a place where I think that if I'm not there that the wheels will fall off. There was ministry and preaching before I showed up and the church will go on after I am gone. I praise God for the lessons learned and I will strive to hold on to what I have learned about God, about the church, and about myself. I commit myself to working to first make God proud and trusting that if I accomplish that goal that self-satisfaction and the satisfaction of the church will not be far behind. Thank God for Field Education because it provides instruction for us as seminarians on how to effectively minister.

Senior Seminar

The year-long course during my senior year called Senior Seminar focused on allowing a safe space from which we could reflect on our journey through seminary. At the beginning of seminary, we all took a course called "Introduction to Church and its Ministry" and this course altered our ideas of ideal ministry. That particular course focused not only on the dos and don'ts of ministry, but that course taught us the importance of self-care and the difficult circumstances in which we would be expected to minister or meet the needs of those in our ministerial contexts. Whereas, the Field Education courses involved practical application of ministry principles, this course was refreshing as we looked back upon the ups and downs of seminary. This class afforded us the opportunity to examine how our modus operandi as well as our philosophy of ministry changed. To that end, this course required the completion of three papers that I desired to share. The full substance of these papers follows.

Response Paper

1. What presuppositions of ministry have been addressed, formulated or refined by the seminary experience?

Through the seminary experience several presuppositions of ministry have been addressed, formulated and refined. Before seminary I believed that the preaching and teaching ministry to which I am called required my complete commitment. It was due to this commitment that I was led to attend this institution in order to be further developed and strengthened. Seminary has reaffirmed this assumption about ministry by emphasizing the responsibility of the preacher to be professional. Throughout my time in seminary it was refreshing to hear further instruction in support of the fitness of women to preach the gospel. Part of this was accomplished by learning about the importance of textuality and context when examining the scriptures. At the same time, this experience at the school of theology has refined my understanding of the worship experience in how each part of the experience should present a consistent message. Therefore, to ensure the success of the worship experience the pastor and music (as a subset of the ministry of worship) should be in partnership. Seminary is responsible for providing a context where I have been able to work out my theology and I now am at a place where I believe that ministry must be holistic and not simply limited to delving into spiritual matters. This change in theology has affected the way I preach because now I am compelled to minister to the whole person.

2. What are some possible contexts for ministry with which you have become acquainted?

Prior to arriving at seminary, I was only aware of the church as the principle context for ministry. Others with whom I have been acquainted introduced me to the contexts of prison ministry and street ministry. Since coming to seminary I have become aware of the professional area of pastoral counseling, including chaplaincy, which is practiced in several different contexts. These contexts include medical facilities as well as the armed forces. Also, the mission trips sponsored by faculty members such as Dr. Monica Spencer and Dr. Boykin Sanders have emphasized that other impoverished nations are valuable contexts for ministry. Field education helped me to see that social service agencies are also great places in which persons minister holistically in areas such as counseling, mentoring and tutoring. One of the areas to which I was exposed during this experience that will shape my future is the context of academia where instructors not only teach subjects but engage in ministry that I endeavor to one day join.

3. In what ways are you more or less equipped to practice ministry as a consequence of the studies undertaken?

Through this seminary experience I am more equipped to practice ministry in several ways. My bible courses and theology courses have shaped my theology to the extent that I am no longer satisfied in dealing just with spiritual needs but now I am more equipped to work toward holistic liberation. Through my three preaching courses I have learned three different methods that support my preaching ministry and have made me a more effective preacher. I have also been equipped through the Christian education curriculum which has taught me several ways of being a more creative instructor. Because of seminary I am much more equipped to provide pastoral care and discern how to handle situations even if a situation necessitates referral. Learning about the history of the church has undergirded me so that I am able to keep the ministry of the local church in context. Community formation has aided me in being better suited for ministry by allowing me to engage in self-discovery and by teaching me ways to care for myself so that I can better minister to God's people. Overall, the courses in the curriculum in seminary have equipped me by teaching me what ministry should be about. By correcting my vision seminary has equipped me to see the need in order to meet the need.

Reflection Paper

<u>What is the Pastor's role in counseling members of the church?</u>

To begin, the pastor's role in counseling members of the church largely depends upon the structure of that particular church. The size of the congregation may make it impractical for the pastor to counsel each member of the church. A large congregation may also elect to hire someone to head a pastoral counseling ministry to handle the bulk of the counseling needs of the church. However, even in such a case the pastor has a role in counseling members of the church even if this must be limited to counseling only the leadership of the church and empowering them to counsel others. The pastor also must be able to discern when she or he is unequipped to handle certain situations so that she or he can refer such situations out of the church. The pastor should not be expected to possess all the answers and should not be expected to be able to fix every issue for which members seek counseling. The aims of the pastor should include healing, sustaining, guiding and reconciling.

Ultimately, the pastor is responsible for providing all sorts of counseling services to the congregation and should at the least provide counsel for others who address the majority of the counseling needs of the church. With regard to specific examples of services, the pastor must provide pre-marital counseling in order to enlighten those who are entering into marriage concerning the challenges of marriage and in order to provide tips on how to make a marriage work. Similarly, the pastor must provide marital counseling so that marriages that are in trouble can perhaps be rescued through the facilitation of effective communication between the spouses (healing and sustaining). Along these lines, the pastor's role in counseling also includes the ability to resolve conflict when persons approach the pastor for the purpose of mediation (healing and reconciliation) and to provide general counseling services geared toward advising and encouraging the membership of the church (guiding).

My journey through the School of Theology has exposed me to various things that the pastor should keep in mind when seeking to counsel members of the church and these things also contribute to a working definition of the role of the pastor in counseling. The pastor in counseling others, for example, should treat the person as being more important than the problem and should promote the premise that the member's relationship with God is more important than finding a solution to the problem. Within the actual counseling session, the pastor's role primarily should be that of an active listener who is not only awaiting an opening to speak but being attentive to the words and feelings of those being counseled. In addition, the pastor should follow the steps of the listening sequence including attending behavior (such as assuming a posture facing those being counseled), asking open and closed questions, and being attentive to the verbal and nonverbal communication. Arguably the most critical of skills for the pastor to possess, especially with regard to care, is to be able to excel in the ministry of presence because this communicates the importance of those seeking care to the pastors providing care. Simply setting aside time to be with the persons for whom pastors provide care speaks volumes about a pastor's love and concern for them.

The pastor also should ensure that she or he seeks to have her or his own counseling needs met. Each pastor working toward the healing, sustaining, reconciling and guiding of membership also has the same needs that need to be address in part because of the virtue that she or he expends in the pastoral care of others. Just as the pastor should encourage those who need counseling to seek it, the pastor must also be willing to see it for herself or himself in order for the pastor to be as whole as possible. In providing care for others and seeking care for themselves, pastors should align with the Hippocratic Oath and do no harm to others or themselves both in the practice of care and the practice of self-neglect.

Senior Assessment Paper

As I approach the finish line of my journey at the Samuel DeWitt Proctor School of Theology I am grateful for the opportunity to stop and reflect on such a life-altering experience. In spite of the difficulties I have encountered along the way and the cost associated with attending, both in terms of finances and time, it is difficult to imagine what might have been had I not answered the call to attend this institution. Each of the courses and instructors has shaped me in their own unique ways and I am indebted to God for directing me to trust this process. In assessing my overall experience as I move closer to graduation I will discuss what I have learned, my personal transformation and my future ministry focus as one who has been blessed to matriculate at STVU.

While the parameters of this paper forbid discussing in detail all that I have learned while enrolled here at STVU, I would like to reflect on what I have learned while resisting the temptation to go into extraneous details. For the sake of clarity my thoughts are grouped on the basis of subject matter rather than being arranged in the order taken. To begin, the curriculum of STVU truly enlightened me with regard to the church and what the church is supposed to be. In this vein, I learned that the purpose of the church and its ministry according H. Richard Niebuhr is to help individuals to grow in their love for one another and for God. The introductory course on the church and its ministry helped me to remember many things, such as the importance of self-care in ministry, which will aid me as I move forward in ministry. Prior to coming to STVU I had a very limited view of what the church should do and what its ministry should entail but I am grateful for improved understanding in this regard. I am also very thankful for the instruction I received in the area of music and worship in the African American church. This course increased my appreciation for the history of the African American church musical tradition. It also opened my mind to the partnership that needs to take place between pastor and music department leader.

In addition to these things, STVU also helped me to understand the importance of and the ideal approach to church administration and finance. The first course taught me what I need to know about leadership and management so that I can be more effective in my areas of responsibility with regard to administration. This is an area of which I would classify myself as a novice and so I cannot overlook the significance of the opportunity to learn more about this part of the church as it allowed me to see the connection between effective church administration and problem solving within the church. Even as I compose this assessment, I am taking a course on church administration and finance. I have already learned much with regard to how the church should handle its business and the role that the pastor and/or church business administrator plays in managing the King's business as Dr. William Whitaker would say.

One of the areas that influenced me most was the area of church history. The courage and faith of martyrs along with the doctrinal struggles that have not disappeared in the millennia since are a couple of the things that resonated with me most. This instruction has affected how I treat those with whom I disagree. It has helped me to see the necessity of treating their views with respect especially when viewed through the lens of the treatment of those who suffered after church persecution turned inward. Reading the primary sources of theologians and church leaders assisted me in broadening my perspective and showing me that there are more shades of gray than I originally considered such as with the topic of original sin. I praise God not only for the material but for the vessel of Dr. Adam Bond who was instrumental in getting me to see my potential in the area of academia. These courses also taught me how to do research and add conversation partners in my dialogue with primary and secondary sources in doing scholarly research.

The instruction I received on the subject of preaching has aided me more than I imagined when I first arrived at STVU. Initially I was arrogant enough to believe that I did not need assistance in method but instruction on biblical studies in order to improve my sermonic material. I cannot conceive of a time when I have been more wrong. This school blessed me tremendously in giving me the tools of the correlation method, the dialectic method and the application method of preaching. Now I feel that I am ever more equipped to preach even the most difficult of texts using one of these models. The first course helped me appreciate the connection between the preaching moment and the planning of the entire worship experience. The second course aided me in seeing the importance of textual interpretation by having to interpret non-biblical texts. The third course showed me that there is room for my personality and poetic inclinations within each sermon. As the result of these courses taken at STVU my preaching ministry will never be the same.

The curriculum of the School of Theology helped transform my thinking further in the areas of biblical studies. Coming into the school I had a very conservative outlook on the nature of the bible and the nature of its inspiration and canonization. However upon leaving STVU my view of the bible has evolved and I could not be more indebted to the school for the enlightening instruction of Dr. Franklin, Sandy Rogers and Dr. Kim. I am thankful in particular for the clarity I received regarding biblical inconsistencies knowing that I no longer need to seek to explain them away but I can embrace them for what they are. The Introduction to Biblical Studies course helped me to understand the importance of exegesis and biblical criticism and this has changed the way I view biblical studies. This course also blessed me in the sense that it enlightened me to better tools that I could use for the purpose of exegesis and study including the scholarly dictionaries, commentaries, the New Revised Standard Version of the bible and the New Interpreter's Bible. The Old Testament course gave me a greater appreciation for Jewish culture and history while also showing me that it was much more complex than I had originally thought. This course increased my love for the Old Testament and for its applications even for today. The New Testament course also provided me with a greater understanding of and gratitude for the gospels and for the Pauline epistles. This course also helped me comprehend the perspectives of the writers of each of the books and continued the conversation about textual criticism (i.e. undisputed Paul, deutero-Paul and the Pastoral Epistles which were likely not written by Paul).

Another area in which I had little or no experience or formal instruction prior to attending STVU was the area of pastoral care. The classes that we took made me aware of the diverse set of occupations and positions within this discipline and of the fact that pastoral care is more about function than a church pastoral position. These classes equipped me with a larger grasp of the complexity and the responsibility of pastoral counseling leaving me thankful for the new skills I have acquired through these courses. An area critical in its own right and related to the sphere of pastoral care is the area of Christian ethics. Once again I came to know that there are many more gray areas than I imagined. While some moral absolutes exist I am grateful for the understanding that immoral does not necessarily mean unethical. This aided me in reexamining some convictions including the position likely held by the majority of the church concerning gay adoption. The traditional view seems to be that such parents are unethical simply on the basis of their behavior being judged as immoral. In addition, this particular class sobered me with regard to all I have to lose as a minister of the gospel if I engage in unethical behavior.

Specifically in the area of finance, I am cautious concerning the appeal of corruption especially after doing an independent study of wealth and poverty in New Testament times. This course revealed that money can be a very strong source of corruption on the evidence of the relationships between New Testament era sectarian convictions concerning wealth and poverty and the economic position of these sects. On a different note, being instructed in the area of Christian education empowered me to be a more effective instructor by enlightening me as to other methods for approaching the teaching task. As the result of having taken this class I will continue to remember the importance of alternating methods for presenting and engaging with material for the purpose of retaining the attention of my students. However, perhaps the portion of my classes that inspires me the most to this day is systematic theology. I enjoy working through the different positions and the rationales for these positions. These courses helped me to evolve in terms of not only what I believe but also strengthened my ability to explain my beliefs. I was also fortunate to take a class on Christology and as a result I am able to define and explain what I believe concerning Christ. In this vein, I am equipped to explain my positions on the ontology of Jesus Christ and what I believe concerning the various atonement theories. Through many of these classes the inclusion of group assignments helped me learn more of what it takes to be an effective leader as well as what it takes for the church (a large group) to work together in order to achieve stated goals. All of these courses had an impact on my convictions, life and ministry.

Now I would like to transition into reflecting on how I have been transformed during my journey in the areas of my beliefs, my character and my approach to ministry. As the result of my sojourn in this institution my views have evolved tremendously. In addition to the items discussed previously, my conservative view of the bible and of salvation has dissipated in favor of a bibliology more in tune with biblical scholarship and a salvation that has much less clearly defined boundaries. In other words, I no longer see the value in using the bible to demonize anyone. Similarly, having learned the context of John 14:6, I also no longer see any value in possessing my former ecclesiastical arrogance in assuming that all non-Christians are destined for hell. While I believe that Jesus is the way, I can no longer seek to assume God's position and speak in absolutes concerning these matters. Currently it is more of a priority to label social sin and indifference than it is for me to label individual sins and demonize persons for things that are essentially between them and God. Near the end of my journey, I now also subscribe to the view that ministry should be holistic and address the needs of the whole person. This belief influences my approaches to teaching and preaching. Formerly I held that spiritual salvation was the only thing that mattered but having been exposed to persons like Walter Rauschenbusch and others I now see that ministry must address other areas of need. These changes in my convictions, among others, have humbled me more than I could have imagined.

Transformation has also become apparent in my approach to ministry. Specifically my modus operandi for counseling, preaching and teaching has changed dramatically. Having a greater appreciation for the level of effort necessary to not only function effectively but to practice these disciplines correctly has modified my approach. Now, I address these tasks with a greater sense of gravity for the extent to which I may help or hinder others in their search for and relationship with God. This process has also made me more reflective in my method so that I seek to gauge the impacts and effects of ministry when planning for ministry events. My attitude toward ministerial tasks has also changed in the sense that I approach each task of ministry with more humility in the sense that I never assume that I can get by on the strength of my gifts alone. I now realize how much I know but am humbled and sobered by the extent to which I remain ignorant when considering all that I still do not understand.

As one who has studied here at STVU, my future ministry foci will include the areas of the church pastoral ministry and the area of the academy. With regard to a future pastoral ministry I aim to utilize all that I have learned to educate those in my pastoral context and to empower them with some of the tools that I have acquired. I will also strive to have a preaching and teaching ministry above reproach and to be the change that I want to see in the kingdom and the world at large. In this pastoral ministry I will seek the holistic wellbeing of the persons whom I am privileged to pastor. In addition as pastor I will utilize all that I have learned in the realms of pastoral care and church administration. Along with this pastoral focus, in the future I will also seek a Doctor of Ministry and at least a singular Ph.D. for the purpose of being able to add my voice to the conversations of scholarship specifically in the areas of systematic theology, homiletics, or church history. At the same time, I desire to teach at the university or seminary level so that I can help others in their struggle while learning what I have been blessed to learn while enduring the process in the school of theology.

I have indeed been blessed by my experience and would not take anything for my journey. Each of the courses contributed in some way to my journey and helped me develop into the person that I am today. I praise God for the privilege of being in this place and space for such a time as this. I am grateful for the instructors and the Dean for all that they have contributed in building a program that empowers its students to this extent. Because of God's grace exhibited in this place I am leaving prepared for the next challenge but also barely recognizing the theology of the person who arrived at orientation almost three years ago. It is also because of this place that I am clear about where I go from here and am excited about where God will take me next. For Senior Seminar, I am also thankful for the opportunity to take time and reflect at the end of this process through this assessment. I hope to be able to invest in something that has blessed me in the future by contributing finances as well as scholarship. To God be the glory, there is no place like Union.

Church Administration

In addition to the year-long courses taken during seminary which focused on practical ministry, during my second year of seminary I took a mandatory course in Church Administration. As previously mentioned, this course taught us the importance of administration and leadership for the success of ministry in the church ministry context. In this course, we discussed hot button issues that affect the leadership of the church to include the role of the diaconate and tithing. Regarding the former, this was always a sensitive subject while in seminary because whenever a hypothetical scenario of friction in the church was necessary, fellow students and professors always used the example of the problematic deacon. This is an issue for me because my father is a deacon, and various individuals have attempted throughout the years to pit him against the pastor and vice versa.

I raised the issue of tithing during one lecture in particular when I felt that many of my classmates, who are pastors, simply held on to the notion of tithing as a means to predict church income and utilized tithing as a method of control. I believed tithing as a rule to be counterintuitive to the New Testament notion of cheerful giving. I believed and still believe that tithing was a practice instituted for a particular people at a particular time, as a means to ensure that the priests, who had no income or land, as well as the fatherless and widows could have what they needed. To be sure, such social support is still necessary today, but that does not mean that God mandated tithing to the New Testament church. I felt and still feel that the rational that says, "if God did not revoke it, it is still true for us, God's children" to be hollow. Surely, those who are able should financially support the church and prioritize giving as a matter of relationship. The discussion about tithing in class reinforced this, but it also helped me to see that not prioritizing giving put me in a position where I took on debts that prevented me from giving as much as I liked. Prior to taking on excessive debt, I gave above 10% and my aim continues to be to sufficiently support my local church through giving.

The majority of the requirements of this course rested in students' availability during class and participating in class discussions. However, one of the major assignments in this course was a group project where Dr. Jackson expected students to develop documents that govern and establish churches. My group entitled our church "Freedom Baptist Church. Joining me in this group were Rev. Dr. Vonda Batts, Rev. Darrell Hairston, Rev. Joshua King, Rev. Lucy Robertson, and Rev. Monica Teal. The pastor, prophetic in hindsight, was Rev. Dr. Nicholas Meade. While pastoring has been evasive, I did go on to earn my doctorate. One of the things that made this project more difficult was the absence of one of our group members, Rev. King. Tragedy required his attention, and to this day he publicly speaks fondly of our group for putting his name on the group project although circumstances prevented him from having his desired impact. That is part of what seminary is all about: family and having each other's back especially when life throws curveballs.

One of the more impactful assignments of this course, that I chose to share in this work, is my Problem/Solution paper. In this paper, the course led by William Jackson, D.Min., an authority on Church Administration, expected students to examine a problem in their particular church contexts and to arrive at a solution to that problem using the new information we learned about leadership and church administration. I chose to focus on the issue of "Committing All Available Gifts to the Cause." This paper addresses a stubborn problem that exists not just in the church but in many non-profit organization to include my fraternity and others.

"Committing All Available Gifts to the Cause"

Introduction

Many times a problem in today's churches can go unnoticed or unaddressed most likely because the congregation is in denial about the problems or because no one in the congregation feels equipped to provide a solution to this problem. The aim of this paper is to discuss a pressing issue in my local church context that my church has failed to remedy at this time. This work will address the issue in detail, offer a hypothesis for a solution and then thoroughly discuss the specifics with regard to implementing the proposed solution to this pervasive issue.

Contextual Issue

The most pressing issue in my local context seems to be the lack of attendance to and enthusiasm for ministry activities and this has led to a lack of availability on the part of the membership in availing their gifts to the congregation. We have an environment where many people complain about the way things are but not willing to work in order to make things better. My context supports the notion that apathy and non-participation is the curse of the church today.[1] The church needs more people to be involved and yet various approaches appealing to members to participate such as calling them or sending letters have failed to stir them to action.

Our church has an excessive amount of members that are stuck in and refuse to progress from the "Congregation" circle – among Rick Warren's "5 Circles of Commitment" – who need to transition to the "Committed" circle who contribute to the effectiveness of the ministry.[2] In other words, our church is lacking is complete commitment from the human resources of the membership that include the members' knowledge, skills, capabilities, potential and diverse set of assets.[3] I would estimate that large majority of our congregation only wants to contribute in Sunday worship but not elsewhere. Part of this lack of utilization of gifts is due to the falling away of so many people on a generational basis as they leave to go to college.

This has led to a lack of spiritual growth in the congregation. The lack of faithful members has led to a decline in potential candidates for leadership positions. As a result, there are numerous single points of failure throughout the congregation and, in contradistinction to most churches the church of my context is undermanaged in part because we have so few trying to do the work of many.[4] Part of the fallout from this issue is that the limited leader resources that our church has are being overwrought and each leader is forced to wear too many hats in order for the church to function.

Hypothesis

In spite of the difficulties in my context, there is hope for a solution to this problem. It is my hypothesis that in order to fix this problem, interpersonal relationships must be improved and a leadership and management training program must be established. This solution to the issue in my local context was not formulated without a specific rationale. To begin, the reason for nurturing interpersonal relationships and for fostering and encouraging friendships is because "friendships at church and congregations that facilitate them are highly correlated with spiritual depth and the desire for ongoing spiritual maturity" and the church leadership should create a culture of "loving, intentionally-welcoming friendships."[5] The leadership and management training program will be led by the senior levels of leadership for the sake of credibility and also so that these seasoned leaders can share insights and past experiences that have shaped them.

Education is a necessary foundation for growth. Without proper education into what the church is supposed to be, the members of the body will not function correctly. Establishing the difference between leadership and management would be to ensure that leaders and managers are not operating outside of the intended scope of their respective positions. I agree with the assessment that "the reason for leadership and guidance in a church is to equip the church. To equip the church is to furnish it for service or action" and this makes more ministry possible.[6] The titles and leadership opportunities exist for the purpose of doing ministry. The program would enable more people to participate in executing the purpose of the church which is "the increase among men of the love of God and neighbor."[7] The program would train leaders and managers because both need to be "included as valued contributions within" the church and each is "necessary for ministry effectiveness."[8] By focusing on empowerment, this program can "reap the human harvest" of these efforts as it provides effective leadership for my local context.[9] The program is a way to get people in the congregation from being apathetic to the vision of the local and universal church to having commitment by communicating the vision and empowering them to enact the vision.[10]

The reason that we need to educate about the connection between membership and commitment is because people will be committed to a church that has high expectations and that expects their contribution to make a difference.[11] Part of what needs to take place is that leadership needs to refocus so that our leaders "instill vision, meaning and trust in their followers" and so that the leaders in the church consciously help everyone to feel wanted and needed by the church.[12] It is a way whereby the church can show that it recognizes the "specialness of people" so that each individual member is regarded and treated with dignity and a sense of worth that he or she deserves.[13]

There is a need in my context for the church to point to people's self-worth and celebrate that they have something to contribute. The program would be a form of actualization – an actualizer is a "person who appreciates himself and his fellowman as persons of worth created in the image of God with unique gifts and abilities."[14] Part of the goal of the program would be to help them understand their potential in order to better discover and fulfill their life's purpose. This program would strive to provide a framework for actualization so that participants will become self-actualizing and end up more committed even without someone else motivating them. This is because when a person is self-actualizing, he or she has commitment that is unyielding and so the problem of commitment is solved when the church actualizes people they are committed and empowered to help solve problems outside of themselves.[15]

When people have a sense of responsibility, they most likely would be more willing to commit themselves further. If they are given a chance on the premise that one day they may be allowed to lead, it would encourage them to become more committed. Another reason why I believe this to be a good solution to the problem of my context is because studies have shown that in order to keep churches growing and effective, one of the things that has to happen is for strong leadership to come from the pastor, staff and leadership.[16] When this happens the ministry has a clear sense of purpose and direction and an emphasis is placed on "increasing numbers of laypersons in carrying out ministries of service."[17] In other words, this program is likely exactly what my local context requires.

Proposed Solution

The first part of my proposed solution addresses interpersonal relationships among the members of the congregation while the second part focuses on a method to empower and invigorate interest into leading the church in the right direction. To facilitate individual relationship growth among the parishioners that should be some type of communication about the common interests of the parishioners. For example, commitment in the church can be fostered if friendships are formed based on the mutual interest in some secular activity like sports or fishing but the mutual interests should not be discriminatory based on a person's economic condition (i.e. anything that is cost-prohibitive because inclusion is the central premise). The second part of this solution includes the creation of a "Leadership and Management Training Program" which would serve to train people to be primarily a part of the volunteer group as opposed to hired staff.[18] The purpose of this program would be to equip people for leadership and management roles within the church as a means to get more committed to serving the church and the larger community.

The proposed curriculum of such a program would include things that are deemed to be critical in the training of leaders. One of the first things that the program will emphasize is the connection between discipleship and commitment, and how as part of one's discipleship he or she should be willing to be used in God's service. The opportunity to be committed to a leadership position must be preceded by a demonstrated effort to live life in an ethical manner. Robert Greenleaf articulated that "legitimate power has become an ethical imperative" signifying a connection between ethics and leadership, and this will help the trainees understand that in order to be effective in leadership and management that one's ethics have to be impeccable.[19] The importance of commitment must be stressed in these sessions. The sessions would communicate to current and potential leaders and managers that being in leadership and management is all about commitment just like salvation is all about commitment. The definition of belief or according to the Apostle Paul is trust and commitment and they are two sides to the same coin.[20] The church has to be clear that membership is for the purpose of working to glorify God and edify the body of Christ. These truths of discipleship should be communicated in the leadership and management training as well as in the packet for new members as they go through new membership classes.

Each session would remind all attendants of the purpose of the church so that they can understand that church administration and leadership is a means to the end of service. The program would have a time to review the church vision and mission statement and communicate how the individual mission of each ministry fits into that. The program would help potential leaders understand the concept of church administration and how it is a means to serve rather than the end (find source, look at definitions of church administration from notes/books). Part of the curriculum for the leadership academy would include clear job definitions for each leadership role in the church so they could have an understanding for what they would be interested in but interest alone would not guarantee a leadership position.

The program would define the distinction between managers and leaders. The distinction could be made this way: "Managers are people who do things right and leaders are people who do the right thing. The difference may be summarized as activities of vision and judgment-effectiveness –versus activities of mastering routines-efficiency."[21] All participants will be taught the skills or strategies of leadership used by many successful leaders such as attention through vision, meaning through communication, trust through positioning, and the deployment of self through positive self-regard and the Wallenda factor.[22] The participants would also be taught about the strategies for motivating people so that each leader is in the process of training other leaders by the example they set.

With regard to the logistics of the training sessions, let me begin by stating that the teaching sessions should be led by the pastor or a deacon since we do not have a church administrator. This training should happen throughout the year so as to provide an opportunity to provide this "basic, preservice leadership training for potential leaders."[23] Sitting leaders should sit in for review and to affirm what they should already be practicing while potential leaders are required to sit through this training before they can assume a leadership position. The training can take place as frequently as demand necessitates. Sitting leadership should be required to take part at least once every six months. Leaders will be required to be managers before assuming a leadership role so that they can pay their dues or do some dirty work so that they will be able to appreciate their managers. At the same time, before members can assume management roles they must have spent at least six months following others management and leadership. The reason that aspiring leaders would need to be managers first is because one has to learn how to follow before he or she can lead.[24] Part of the message is that in times where one is not leading, at least in a formal position, that he or she can

Practical 125

lead by example and follow others the way that he or she would want them to follow. This mirrors the golden rule of the gospel.

One's availability and opportunity to serve will be in part based on the review of one's previous management or leadership experience and an evaluation of how interested persons have performed in following the leadership or management of others. The only exceptions to these policies would be in the case of sitting leadership at the inception of the program. In the cases of new membership, taking the leadership training would not be sufficient to garner a leadership position but would also be contingent on the guidance from the pastor as to how long a person should be a member before becoming eligible to become an official leader in the church. So, the process doesn't become political, the names of interested parties should be submitted to the pastor for ultimate approval.

Upon completion of the first training session, an action plan will need to be executed in order to implement further changes to the church's leadership structure. To begin interested and persons approved by the pastor would have to undergo more specific evaluation and training for roles in the leadership offices of deacon and trustee. Next, the new levels of leadership would have to be established in the form of management offices under the guidance of each ministry leader not for the purpose of adding complexity but to provide for more delegation of duty. Each ministry leader will be liberated to serve as the visionary for that particular ministry and would be concerned about doing the right thing and trusting others to do it the right way. The leader will be able to lead with vision and see the big picture. For example, in the women's ministry it could have a manager to manage a group for single women, a group for married women and a group for mothers who could offer more specific management for the unique issues faced by the more specific demographic under each ministry. With regard to tenure, I believe that the management of these groups should be rotated out for diversity and to give others an opportunity to exercise their leadership skills. Periodically this training program must be reviewed and changed to increase effectiveness and efficiency.

Conclusion

This paper has identified the problem of commitment in my local context and has proposed a leadership and management training program as a way to solve this problem. It has also discussed why, of all the solutions I could have chosen, I chose this particular solution. It is my hope that my local church will have a fruitful discussion of both the present facts as well as our future hope in regard to the commitment of the membership. If this is to happen, we as a local church body cannot afford to put our heads in the sand and ignore the problem but move forward in trusting God and each other so that we may effectively lead and manage God's business.

---

[1] McDonough, 1.
[2] Warren, 130.
[3] Tidwell, 127.
[4] Shawchuck and Heuser, 23.
[5] Lindsay, 39.
[6] Tidwell, 28.
[7] Niebuhr, *The Purpose of the Church and its Ministry*, 31.
[8] Shawchuck and Heuser, 22.
[9] Bennis and Nanus, 74.
[10] Shawchuck and Heuser, 150-151.
[11] Murrow, 161.
[12] Bennis and Nanus, 7.
[13] Tidwell, 126.
[14] McDonough, 36.
[15] Ibid., 125.
[16] Shawchuck and Heuser, 114.
[17] Ibid.
[18] Tidwell, 128.

[19] Shawchuck and Heuser, 15.
[20] Ehrman, "The Gospel according to Paul: The Letter to the Romans," 360.
[21] Bennis and Nanus, 20.
[22] Ibid., 25.
[23] Tidwell, 132.
[24] Williams, 134.

4

Theological

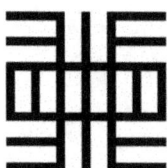

One of the more impactful elements of my sojourn through seminary includes time spent wrestling with my theology or what I believe about God. Seminary introduced me to the inner workings and complex world of systematic theology. Mostly fundamentalist upon entering seminary, my theology evolved through the years and seminary provided me with the tools to articulate my personal theology. Such changes in my theology continue to guide my preaching and teaching. The curriculum served its purpose to not only challenge what I believed but armed me with the ability to understand what I believe and why. It reinforced the notion that we need to spend time wrestling with our theology and interrogating our theology with hard questions if our theology is going to stand up against the challenges of our world. If God is at the center of our world, how we see God impacts every facet of our lives and worldviews.

I appreciate the opportunities given in my two courses of systematic theology along with my senior course in Christology. During my first course in systematic theology, I defined theology. I wrote "Theology is the study of those things that motivate persons to reflect on their identity and the meaning of life and motivates them to live a moral life because the ultimate concern in staying true to that motivating factor, i.e. God." At some other time in the course I defined theology differently, writing, "Theology is the study of how God brings hope and ultimate meaning to life and how God requires persons to live their lives for God's approval and conduct their lives in an ethical manner that reflects the belief that this life is not all that there is." Theology is extremely important. In this course, groups made group presentations about different types of theology to include womanist theology, prosperity theology, narrative theology and Pentecostal theology (my group). We had intense discussions as we wrestled with what we believed and why.

Normally, Dean Kinney would teach students in Systematic Theology II. However, that year he had some health challenges and he could not teach as expected. While disappointed, the school blessed us by appointing Dr. Faith Harris to teach in his absence. She challenged our thinking as well as her assignments, to include an ethnography, focused on correlating beliefs with our lived experience in our ministerial contexts. Our work led us to examine why we do some of the things we do and say some of the things we say in worship. She showed us that theology is everywhere and inescapable. If one wants to know what people in the church believe, one only must observe and listen to the language and customs exhibited during worship and other activity. This is true because the formative factors of theology include reason, tradition, scripture, and experience. The ethnography prepared me to do research as part of my Doctor of Ministry program as I had to collect data in the form of observations and complete verbatims for interviews in my doctoral research. I am grateful for the introduction to action research.

To provide insight into the evolution of my theology, this work includes three of my theological papers. Each of these works contributed to my success in these courses. The other paper included in this chapter is my theology of preaching. Now follows my theological statement, which precedes my theology of preaching, before this chapter concludes with my Christology paper. I wrote first and last of these papers in courses taught by Rev. F. Todd Gray who is very knowledgeable and who challenged us to think deeper. Aside from our theological statements, Christology required group projects that focused on H. Richard Niebuhr's *Christ & Culture*—a profound theological work. The middle paper originated from my second-year preaching course. These papers follow.

Theological Statement

Introduction

The content of this paper is intended to articulate my personal theology. To accomplish this goal, a definition of theology or the hermeneutical lens through which I interpret things such as events both past and present. The paper will then move to qualify or in some cases define the four formative factors of theology including scripture, experience, reason, and tradition and will explain how these particular factors have influenced and still influence my definition of theology. Following this, space will be given to compare and contrast two theological paradigms based on my definition of theology.

Definition of Theology

First, a definition for theology consistent with my perspective and values must be established. Based on what is important to me, theology is the study of God and how the knowledge and power of God leads to spiritual liberty that is paramount but also holistic liberation for persons in the face of all the types of bondage that humanity encounters. This liberty is evidenced by the abilities of persons who have had an encounter with God to live lives consistent with God's character and expectations who are free and who do not view God's standard as another form of bondage but helpful guidelines from a loving Father to a child. My definition of theology seeks to reconcile the identity and character of God with all goes on in the world and it seeks to identify ways and areas in which the church universal can minister and meet the holistic needs of humanity.

Formative Factors

My definition of theology has been shaped by the four formative factors of scripture, experience, reason and tradition. While there may be some overlap between them, each category separately has shaped my definition of theology and as these formative factors or my perception or understanding of them change, my definition of theology must change with it. First, there is the formative factor of scripture. As a Christian believer, scripture for me is limited to the protestant canon of the Bible. Hereafter when I mention scripture I am referring to only the contents of the sixty-six books of the Bible. I believe that the Bible is inspired in the sense that it is authoritative in the lives of Christian believers because it still provides a narrative, among other things, of people in relationship with God. The theory of plenary verbal inspiration or that the writers of the bible took dictation is inconsistent with what I know about scripture. I reject the notion of inerrancy because I believe that over the years especially during times where scripture was hand-copied that errors had to have been introduced. Due to my views on the inspiration and inerrancy of scripture, I do not view the scripture as being authoritative in a sense of being literally interpreted but that Christians must pay attention to the contextual lesson of the text and seek to know its relevance for today.

Scripture has shaped my definition of theology because of its content. For example, scripture holds the gospel or good news about the birth, life, ministry, death and resurrection of Jesus Christ who is my Lord. The stories of scripture have shaped my definition of theology because they have taught me much about the character of God. While I will not go as far as Marcion, who believed that the God of the Old Testament was contradistinctive to the God of the New Testament who sent Jesus, I do believe that God is portrayed in a way consistent with Yahwistic propaganda in the Old Testament. To that end while scripture testifies to the power of God to do the impossible (Luke 1:37), I do not accept the notion that God is a God who sanctions genocide. I do however, ascribe to the belief that scripture has taught me that God gives grace. It is scripture through the use of narratives and psalms among other literary forms that has shaped my definition of theology in the sense that it has led me to believe in the attributes of God that scripture portrays such as God's omnipotence, omnipresence, omniscience, sovereignty, and immutability. Without scripture, I would never have received a foundation on which to build a relationship with God post-encounter. Not only this, but scripture has shaped my definition of theology due to the imperatives in the text to minister to people holistically based on the premise that God blessed in various ways in the biblical text and that God never sanctioned permanent brokenness. Especially in the ministry of Jesus Christ, the biblical text shows God desires for persons to be whole through the performance of miracles. My definition of theology is shaped by the narratives in the Bible that portray over and over again the "timeless themes of a people's liberation, continuing resistance to oppression, and quest for social equality."

In addition to scripture, the formative factor of experience has also shaped my definition of theology. This includes both the experience of my ancestors and my personal experience over these first thirty years of my life. The liberating power of God as evidenced through the liberation of my people from slavery has given form to my definition of theology in part because now I know that no matter how bad things look God is able to turn things around. It has taught me that any enduring bondage and oppression is subject to God's power and that just like the Exodus narrative I believe God heard the cry of my people in this country. Experience has taught me that God is still a God that desires wholeness for everyone and not simply for those who embrace the Christian faith. Through the premature birth of my son God has shown me that God is able to heal no matter what it looks like. Through the death of grandfather when I was only seven years old God has shown an ability to give me peace and comfort. Through all the times that my family struggled financially until the point where my family of origin was able to purchase a house and move to the suburbs God showed me that God cares about my needs. My life's story is littered with examples of how God has been all that I have needed God to be. This is part of the reason why my definition of theology has been molded into a shape that accepts holistic ministry as God's design for the world.

My personal narrative has taught me that God desires intimacy and this includes honesty. On one particular occasion, I was honest with God and told God that I felt that if God did not rescue me from something then I would have no other recourse than to lie and try to get myself out of it. Before I could fix my mouth to lie, God had already worked it out and this showed me that God transcends my issues. This particular story does not mean that I believe God is able to be manipulated or extorted but it shaped my definition of theology by showing me that God is available and that God cares about all of me and not simply the spiritual. Through the blessings of my wife and children, God used my experience to shape my definition of theology and now I know that God will answer prayer, regardless of the answer, and is willing to provide the necessary guidance and assistance just as a good father or mother does for his or her child. However, having grandparents die of cancer has shaped my definition of theology so that it now reflects the fact that while God has the power to change things God will not always intervene but my definition of theology says that God knows best.

At the same time, reason has also shaped my definition of theology. Most of the time reason or logic has aided in the formation of my definition of theology through the interpretation of my experience or through grappling with scripture. I came to seminary as a fundamentalist but I know that before I leave many of my hardline stances will have been softened if not eliminated. Reason has shaped my definition of theology because I have had to use reason in seeking to find answers to some hard questions relating to my pre-seminary theology. I have had to ask questions of scripture such as "I know this is possible, but is this probable?" and have found that one needs to have reason to go along with faith to make sense of some things. For instance, there are some things such as a dead man being raised from the dead that offends my sense of logic or reason but I can explain some of these similar issues as being matters of faith but not all. Reason has allowed me to see that while scripture is authoritative I also need reason to be a part of the equation. For example, through my Old Testament studies and using extra-biblical sources I have seen that many things that I was taught to accept as history cannot be logically accepted now because unbiased interpretation of other sources casts serious doubt on these events such as the exodus of millions of Hebrews according to the Torah.

No longer do I view it necessary to leave my mind at the door when entering the realm of biblical studies and reason has shaped my definition of theology by encouraging me to focus on what matters in the scripture instead of being fanatical about disputed details. No longer is God the God who created the world necessarily according to the creation myths of the book of Genesis but reason also dictates that it does not make sense for all of this to come into existence by chance without some initiator of the process. Reason has shaped my definition of theology in the sense that I understand that my mind is finite and incapable of being wrapped around an infinite God. But in the sense of holistic ministry, reason has given form to my definition of theology because it does not make sense that God would care only about the spiritual and want the world to languish in other areas. That since I believe God has purpose for all of us, part of that is in helping toward a common good knowing that just because one is whole spiritually does not mean that person is whole because the spiritual is only one part of each individual. I reject the premise of enlightenment rationalism that says that human reason is sufficient to tell humankind everything it needs to know about God because man is dependent up God's self-revelation to know who God is.

Lastly among the formative factors, my tradition has informed or shaped my definition of theology. Tradition may be defined as those things handed down from previous generations. The fundamentals of the Christian faith are grounded in the transcribed copies of the oral traditions surrounding the good news of Jesus Christ and so in that way tradition provided an introduction to God through Jesus Christ and in doing so established a foundation for my definition of theology. One of the ways in which tradition has formed my definition of theology is through traditional interpretations and understandings of scripture that I have had to unlearn since I have been in seminary. My definition of theology is also partly the result of the tradition as articulated in the scriptures and also a result of the foundational post-protestant reformation theology that is still prevalent in the Baptist church of today including my local church. My home church context is for the most part a fundamentalist context and I would be at the very minimum labeled a heretic if I articulated how my traditional beliefs have had to change in response to enlightenment.

Tradition found in the form of music whether it is through Negro spirituals or hymns have also contributed to my definition of theology. For example, the Negro spirituals shaped my definition of theology to reflect belief in a God who delivered people from bondage and this is part of the reason that I believe in God's ability to provide holistic liberation even today. Common experiences documented in hymns have aided my understanding of the fact that God expects Christians to be more united that we are today. There are also individual experiences that I cannot remember but my parents retell on occasion and these stories reinforce my definition of theology which holds that God is interested in the whole person even when that person is young and/or operating in ignorance. Tradition that shaped my definition of theology has also taken the form of handed down expressions such as "God takes care of fools and babies" and "if you take one step, God will take two." While these expressions have become cliché for the most part they have impacted my definition of theology so that I cannot affirm the condemnation of native peoples that sit in ignorance of the gospel and on the other hand I must reject traditions that have no basis in any other of my formative factors.

Fundamentalism and Liberation Theology
Compare and Contrast

My definition of theology has aspects of both fundamentalism and liberation theology however these two paradigms have been shaped differently and I will discuss them through the hermeneutic of my own theology. Each of these paradigms has a particular view of God and a particular issue that it was formulated to address or solve. In the case of fundamentalism, it sees God as the God of the Bible when interpreted literally and was formulated to address the liberalization of theology due to the introduction of "biblical criticism, evolution and liberal theology" which in the view of fundamentalists constituted a threat to the faith of the church. To solve this problem, fundamentalism called for a return to the literal and traditional understanding of scripture so that persons may be saved from ourselves and the teaching that the founders of fundamentalism rejected. Liberation theology however sees God as being the God on the side of the oppressed and the problem it addresses is oppression in all forms. To solve this problem liberation theology proposes that God's intervention is necessary so that persons may be emancipated from the oppressed. Each paradigm has been shaped by the four formative factors.

First, both fundamentalism and liberation theology have been shaped by scripture. Fundamentalism holds that the Bible was the foundation of the Christian faith and as a result fundamentalists set up Bible institutes to combat the perceived corruption of seminaries. Since scripture is foundational for fundamentalist theology, what fundamentalists believe comes from their interpretations of the Bible including beliefs regarding the virgin birth and deity of Jesus, the substitutionary atonement, the literal, physical resurrection of Jesus and the literal, physical return of Christ. My definition of theology allows for all of these beliefs to be true. On the other hand, liberation theology has been shaped by scripture through the understanding that the Bible presents a case for the liberation of all people. Also, the Exodus, prophetic "denunciation of oppression" and Jesus' ministry to the least of these as articulated in scripture provided foundation support for liberation theology. I embrace the scriptural basis for liberation theology that is also located in the Old Testament concept of "shalom" or wholeness and believe it to be God's desire. These contributions from scripture to the formulation of liberation theology have also shaped my definition of theology that maintains that God cannot possibly be indifferent to the oppression of any particular demographic of persons.

Both fundamentalism and liberation theology have been shaped by experience. Fundamentalism was established primarily as a reactionary movement to reaffirm the importance of scripture. On the other hand, experience continuously reforms my definition of theology and it adjusts appropriately. At the same time, liberation theology arose directly as the result of the "Latin American situation of the 1960s and 1970s." Other forms of liberation theology came to be due to oppression such as black theology in response to the oppression of black Americans in the United States. It was formulated to respond to the experiences of the oppressed. My definition of theology has been partially shaped by the past oppression of my ancestors and so this base of liberation theology has merit.

Now turning to the discussion of how reason informs fundamentalism it follows that since the Bible is the foundation of fundamentalism that through the use of reason fundamentalism rejects anything that would challenge literal interpretations of scripture such as evolution as a challenge to the Genesis creation stories. This is because if it contradicts scripture, common sense directs fundamentalists to reject these challenges because if any part of the integrity of scripture falls then salvific assurance falls with it. My definition of theology affords the possibility that while scripture is a primary authority that other sources should be used to supplement the information and where facts and not theories contradict scripture my definition of theology uses reason to reconcile the two or side with one or the other. My definition of theology agrees with the fundamentalist notion that common sense directs the Christian to emulate Christ in areas of social concern. Common sense also gave shape to liberation theology through the sensible notion that if God cared about the whole person throughout the history of God's interaction with mankind surely God still cares now. The use of praxis, or action and reflection, by the founders of liberation theology also show the importance of reason to help formulate this theology. My definition of theology is consistent with these two aforementioned aspects of liberation theology.

Tradition has also shaped fundamentalism in the sense that it accepts the handed down values of literal interpretation of scripture to the extent that it accepts the Genesis account of creation. While due to formal analysis I disagree with the literal interpretation of these accounts, I do believe the central tenet of that text is that God created the world. Fundamentalism also affirms "the unity and plenary inspiration of scripture." My definition of theology rejects this traditional notion of inspiration due to evidence that at least the Deuteronomic history of the Old Testament was not an inspired piece but a tapestry woven together using different types of sources for the goal of its editor(s). Fundamentalism also maintains the traditional view that the Bible is inerrant and infallible at least in its autographic form and views the Bible as the principle form of God's revelation. While I agree in the authoritative nature of scripture, God is bigger than the Bible and God's interaction with humankind goes beyond what's revealed in the Biblical text. Liberation theology has been shaped by tradition however it has not been established systematically after the "first principles handed down by Christian tradition." The oral traditions recorded in the scriptures shaped liberation theology and informed its perspective that God is on the side of the oppressed. According to my definition of theology, however, God is on everyone's side and not simply the side of the oppressed but I do agree with liberation theology's emphasis on the unity of history and God's activity in all of history.

Conclusion

Care has been given to articulate my definition of theology so that one understands the importance of holistic ministry to me based on my belief in its importance to God. Each formative factor has played a role in the shaping of not only theology but the theological paradigms of fundamentalism and liberation theology. It is my contention that many of us, especially who have been called to trust the process of seminary if we have allowed seminary to go through us, will leave these hallowed grounds with a customized theology that would be impossible to confine to one theological paradigm.

Theology of Preaching

The next paper is my theology of preaching created as part of the requirements for my second-year preaching course with Dr. James Harris. It includes my mindset with regard to what preaching should accomplish particularly with regard to informing and persuading others concerning my theology as revealed and informed by the biblical text. There exists a direct correlation between how one sees God's desires for humanity and the type of preaching in which one engages. Believing, for example, that God is not satisfied until every part of us is free, which informs my preaching in that it focuses on liberation of the hearers to live the life that God wants for them. Conversely, a theology which depicts God as a type of boogey man who is eager to punish. Therefore, others preach messages meant to motivate listeners to act out of fear as opposed to love. Presented below is my theology of preaching.

Introduction

This work will explore a theology for preaching but first it is necessary to explain my understanding of this task. The most basic definition of theology is the study of God and while the definitions for preaching vary I understand a theology of preaching to somehow show the relationship between God and preaching. A theology of preaching, in my estimation, should point out where God is in this business of preaching and how preaching ought to best reflect God's desires the recipients of the preached word. To tackle this task, I will first provide an overview of my own development as a preacher including a description of the influences that have shaped me as a preacher. Then I will define my personal theology that has been shaped by the formative factors of scripture, experience, tradition and reason.[1] I will then define preaching before using my theology as a hermeneutical lens through which the view the preacher's identity, mission, method, and message.

My Development

Experience has taught me that a preacher's theology of preaching is not constructed in a vacuum but is largely influenced by the preacher's narrative and personal development. Like many preachers that have come before me, I have largely been influenced by the preaching of my pastor who has been my pastor for the duration of both my Christian experience and my preaching ministry. It was under the guidance of my pastor, who was largely educated at Liberty University and therefore a theological conservative, that I answered both the call to salvation and to the gospel ministry. The majority of what I knew about preaching when entering the ministry came from sitting under the preaching of my pastor on a weekly basis and it was in this context that I came forth and at least initially largely reflected my pastor's style of preaching.

My pastor's style reflected the time honored tradition of call and response as he would make some claim based in the text, issue some directive for the congregation and then wait to hear the congregation respond in an anticipated manner. He only preached from the King James Version of the Bible and primarily would choose a title for his sermons based on the text that he used. On occasion, however, based on the needs of the congregation he would focus on addressing the pressing issues in the lives of the congregation and would use the text as a pretext. My pastor also is a "Bible-runner" in the sense that while he focuses on one text he often leads the congregation around the Bible to locate and read verses that he gives as evidence to support the claims that he makes. I learned from him that sermons should be both encouraging but challenging and comforting but prophetic. Concerning vocabulary, my pastor has always refrained from using big words so that everyone under the sound of his voice, including children, would be able to understand the crux of what he preached. With regard to style, my pastor is a whooper and so I learned that style is important but never sufficiently substitutes for substance. When it came to structure, my pastor would always have some type of introduction followed by several points of emphasis and then seal his offering with a conclusion. He never used a manuscript but more like a cross between a manuscript and an outline. At the same time, he would often go off-script on tangents as he felt led to do so. His ministry has and still affects the way that I minister when given an opportunity to preach the gospel.

As I previously stated, it was under my pastor's ministry that I answered the call to preach and this took place in May 2003 and I preached my initial sermon on July 6, 2003 at my home church. The selected pericope came from II Corinthians 5:18-20 and Colossians 1:20-21. My subject was "Reconcilable Differences" and it was a kerygmatic message that inferred that all of the difference that exists between sinful humankind and holy God can be overcome through salvation. Much about my first sermon reflected the elements of my pastor's sermons that I mentioned previously. The initial tendency for me to use two separate texts, even one from "undisputed" Paul and the other from Second Paul, reflected my pastor's habit of doing a fair amount of cross-referencing from different texts. Also, the text that I used came from the King James Version of the Bible in the same vein as my pastor. The content of the message was encouraging and challenging and it left the congregation with a sense of hope. I primarily focused on substance as I was unsure of how to vocally present the information. However, I used only a loose outline for this message due to the fact that I knew the sermon so well and I was not familiar with the principle or advantages of using a manuscript to preach. The message itself was structured in the same way that my pastor structured his sermons with the introduction being followed by a series of three points before ending my first foray into the preaching experience. In the end I did not stray from what I had written and I did not whoop in the traditional sense but raised my voice in excitement as I closed the message. In looking back on my initial sermon I can see how much my pastor's style and approach to preaching influenced me even though he nor anyone else ever took the time to actually sit me down and teach me how to write a sermon.

Through the duration of my preaching ministry my writing style has changed. Part of this is due to the evolving example of my pastor but to a larger extent my exposure to more preaching through venues such as the Hampton University Ministers Conference has caused more development of my sermon composition. I began attending the conference in 2007 and this was the first year of the presidential leadership of Dr. William Curtis. Listening to Dr. Curtis and the presenters that have come over the last few years has greatly influenced my writing style because many of them have inspired me to be more careful about my word choices. I noticed that many of the preachers preached from a manuscript and so they were able to know in the preaching moment the exact words that would likely be best used to communicate their message. This forever altered my view that a preacher should preach from an outline and give room for the Holy Spirit to expand the outline in the sermonic moment. This helped me become more refined in what I present especially when it came to telling stories that would help to explain the premises I presented. Also, these preachers and professors have encouraged me to tap into the common heritage of viewing God as the liberator of our people.

I have observed the eloquence and professionalism of these persons and these factors have also contributed to me becoming the preacher I am today. This is because they not only taught me that it is possible to be poetic yet have substance but they have also taught me that professionalism and a sense of confidence in what one is presenting engenders confidence in the hearers. Another venue that has served as a means through which I am able to look at other preachers and glean helpful hints that will help me be effective is the internet through sites such as YouTube and StreamingFaith.com. Using this method I have been inspired by preachers such as Dr. Charles Booth to be prophetic and by preachers such as Pastor E. Dewey Smith to be comfortable in my own skin. My pastor often would share the names of preachers that have influenced him such as A. W. Tozer and Charles Spurgeon among others and so it is likely that in a transitive way I have been influenced as they influenced the preaching ministry of my pastor.

Now I would like to turn to a discussion regarding the sources of information that informed my sermons. My pastor influenced my view on sources because as I stated previously my pastor largely only utilized the King James Version of the Bible but he also used and still uses commentaries extensively. Over the years, his particular commentaries of choice have varied but they have always been a part of his process when writing his sermons. These commentaries included the Matthew Henry Commentary and the Preacher's Outline and Sermon Bible. Early in my preaching experience I relied too heavily on commentaries and had trouble finding my own voice or being comfortable in my own skin. This was partially due to the fact that prior to preaching my initial sermon I had no access to commentaries and so my initial sermon was the sermon that I constructed with the least amount of outside influence or contributions. After I preached my initial sermon I received a few commentaries and in the sermons that would follow I would overuse these sources and consult with them so quickly that I did not give myself the opportunity to encounter the text. Other sources such as the Life Application Study Bible had too much say in the first few sermons that followed my initial sermon. This experience taught me to spend time meditating on the text and to "walk up and down the road of the text" before consulting with sources that would saturate my thought with the opinions of others. This practice still stays with me but I have learned that sermon preparation is a matter of research and therefore, as Dr. Adam Bond says, I need to be able to introduce more conversation partners to this process.

Seminary has developed my sermon preparation because now I am able to practice specific methods of sermon preparation such as the correlation method and the dialectical method. The School of Theology has increased my awareness and utilization of more conversation pieces than I have before. I used to only utilize commentaries but now I have learned to access scholarly journals and articles but I also have learned the power of leveraging other translations than the King James Version. In addition, I have learned the power of using scholarly Bible dictionaries and encyclopedias of Christianity that present facts without attempting to encourage faith. The School of Theology has taught me that there is value in reading the Septuagint and in utilizing interlinear bibles. All of these conversation partners now have a place in my process of crafting a sermon. I am grateful to God that over time my understanding of capable sources for sermons has evolved but I also realize that more growth is necessary.

Time and experience also led to my development with regard to how I present the sermon. I learned early in my ministry that I could not be consumed with people's reactions to what I proclaimed. A mentor of mine impressed upon me to preach the gospel and let the chips fall instead of waiting for people to respond a certain way. This helped me to view success in preaching not in relation to the number of persons shouting but in whether or not God is proud of me. It also helped me to see that I could not be successful in preaching trying to be someone other than who I am. While watching preachers such as Noel Jones, Eddie Long, T.D. Jakes and other preachers on television I observed how each of them was comfortable in their own skin and did not try to be anyone else. I came to realize that if I am authentic to my own identity that this will prevent me from attempting to be like someone else. In addition to the examples of other preachers, the persons in my home church helped me to develop my sermonic presentation because they did not appreciate carbon copies but wanted to be able to see individual approaches and styles among the associate ministers at our church. While there are some who focus on style more than they do substance, the majority of those in my context only affirm those who provide them with substance that can help them rather than simply providing a meal of clichés. Ever since I entered the faith, my father has been a major influence for me and that has not ceased simply because I am a preacher and he is a deacon. He and I routinely discuss theological matters and we often discuss other preachers' sermons. We are in agreement that substance matters more than style and knowing that he is willing to tell me the truth has influenced how I present the sermon. It is not due to the fact that I feel it necessary to impress him but simply because he is a reminder of the fact that the people need more than eloquence – they need sustenance.

In addition to the aforementioned influences, I have also been influenced by my own work in ministry. My experience of leading the young people at my church has helped me to see more of what needs to be addressed from the pulpit and also taught me that a preacher must be informed of what each gene4ration to which he or she ministers is dealing with. Also, my recent experience of serving as a mentor to three preachers relatively new to the call and task has shaped me because it put me in the position where I must be able to explain why I do what I do both in the preparation and presentation of my sermons. All of these factors have contributed to my personal development as a proclaimer of the gospel. I am grateful for everyone and everything that has contributed to the preacher I am today but I am also encouraged that God is not through with me yet.

My Theology

Theology is the study of God and how God moves to facilitate or accomplish both the spiritual and holistic liberation of persons living in all types of bondage. The mark of those who have been liberated spiritually is a concern for the will of God being done on earth and reflects God's dissatisfaction with both spiritual and other forms of bondage. Bondage is anything that keeps one from being all that God intended for humanity to be as exemplified by Christ. God must be a God that not only cares about the spiritual part of us but be the God who is concerned with the whole person. God's character and concern for the whole person should be reflected in all who profess to be God's people. In this sentiment I mirror the thought of Dr. Martin Luther King Jr. who openly questioned the spiritual condition of the white clergy who seemingly embraced spiritual liberty but in their cowardice were disengaged from the bondage of Jim Crowism. A system of preaching that only seeks to liberate spiritually embodies the principle of being so heavenly minded that it is of no earthly good.

Preaching Defined

Preaching is the proclamation of good news of the life, death, and resurrection of Jesus and the good news that now salvation is available to all.[2] It is the declaration of information that is vital for the perseverance of the saints and seeks to communicate the hope for escaping the real that is only possible in God. It has been said that preaching is "truth through personality."[3] With this I agree because while the bible may not be full of facts it certainly communicates truth concerning God. Also, God has chosen individuals with unique experiences and personalities to be the conduits through which the good news comes forth. While this definition is simplistic, it communicates the larger premise that the truth, once known, is able to free persons from bondage. Preaching that communicates the truth of the premise that God is on the side of the oppressed is necessary but not the extent that persons use this premise to manipulate people into stuffing the pockets of preachers who are only interested in monetary gain. I speak of the prosperity gospel that uplifts persons on the faulty foundation consisting of promises of impending wealth. While this gospel puts God on the side of the oppressed it is sorely limited in its presentation of the truth.

Preaching is the presentation of sermons and other definitions for sermons include that of G. Ray Jordan who said that "A sermon is a statement of faith, drawn from the context of tradition, projecting the authentic being of the preacher."[4] Once again, this definition stresses the importance of the individuality of the preacher but it must be joined by a statement of beliefs rooted in tradition. In other words, our understanding of who God is and what we believe about God must be communicated through the sermon and this belief has its foundation in the oral and written traditions of the previous encounters of God with humankind. Since scripture and the faith that has been handed down specifically to those in the black church tradition we view God as the one who has liberated our people from slavery. This is one of the major elements that separate the black church experience from all others and even those traditions who are similar because their faith is rooted in God's liberating work, no experience of bondage is exactly the same. In preaching liberation, the sermon communicates the idea that "there is no secret what God can do" and the liberation that took place for those in the past is yet possible for those who struggle in the present.

One of the things that preaching involves according to David Buttrick is the extraction and exposure of "convictional understandings-understandings of God."[5] This means that preaching shares the character of God of which we are convinced and this includes our persuasion that God is on the side of the oppressed. Preaching is one aspect of ministry which as a whole is designed to effect wholeness. Of ministry, Cheryl Sanders said the following:

> …it is the meaningful progress toward human wholeness that occurs when men and women emulate Christ and undertake his mission of bringing the reign of God to bear upon all aspects of human existence.[6]

In other words preaching should work toward the wholeness of all mankind beginning with spiritual salvation. "The missiological emphasis of the black church must focus on solidarity, survival, and wholeness" to J. Deotis Roberts and this means the preachers that lead these churches must preach in support of these aims especially that of wholeness.[7] More about this is covered in the section to follow that deals with our motive for preaching.

Identity: Who Must the Preacher Be?

The preacher should be one who has been called to preach although it has been said that this is more of a conviction than an indisputable fact.[8] The preacher is, by nature, dialectic. He or she is constantly in a struggle between the ideal self and the real self. If the preacher would proclaim the truth the preacher also must be willing to embody the truth. It is not sufficient to simply present words of encouragement and platitudes about God's caring nature. In the sobering words of Mahatma Gandhi as preachers "We must be the change that we seek."[9] A preacher must be willing to get his or her hands dirty and actually give the effort to produce the holistic nature that is sorely needed. This means that preach must be one who is willing to preach with his or her voice and also preach through his or her way of life in service to others. This is because "the life of the speaker has greater weight in determining whether he is obediently heard than any grandness of eloquence."[10] The preacher must be one who by nature is willing to sacrifice of himself or herself in the preacher's freedom in order to work for another's freedom.

The contribution of the preacher to holistic liberation of persons must begin with the mission to be a messenger "of hope for the oppressed and be concerned about social injustice."[11] According to Samuel D. Proctor being a social prophet, who also recognizes the necessity of comfort and religious education, is one of the roles that the preacher must fulfill and this means having the courage to be critical of society.[12] This does not mean that the preacher can always liberate persons but we can be, as Jerry Carter described, "a quivering mass of availability – not to meet needs to but help others discover the needs that need to be met"[13] We can do so with the understanding that it is the Son who makes people free.[14] This is impossible unless the preacher is aware of the issues that people are struggling with. The preacher must be one who is aware of his or her "social, political, educational, and economic surroundings" because each of these areas is infiltrated by bondage.[15] The type of empathy that makes preaching effective can only be offered by the preacher "who lives among the people and who sits where the people sit and know of their struggles and heartaches and bad experiences."[16]

The preacher must also be one who is self-aware and this is only possible through the practice of continual self-understanding.[17] This means being understanding of the premise that the preacher is dialectic and that the preacher is subject to bondage also. Sexual and material bondage have been the causes of the downfalls of some preachers. Other forms of bondage pervade not only the pew but the pulpit as well. The preacher must be one who is willing to live with a certain level of transparency and honesty about his or her fallibility. Brad Braxton echoed this sentiment when he encouraged preachers to active in "embracing our shadow side."[18] Put another way, Gardner Taylor in his lectures acknowledged that we as preachers have "humbling negatives."[19]

The preacher must be one who is Holy Spirit led and empowered if he or she expects to be a blessing to those who are experiencing bondage by speaking the word of God. The same Holy Spirit that empowers us to preach is the same Spirit who called us to this sacred vocation.[20] I echo the sentiments of the "Harvard Hooper" Charles G. Adams who said "it is my deepest desire that the Holy Spirit will mandate, motivate, generate and articulate good news to all people through my poor, lisping, stammering tongue."[21] While his description may have been hyperbole and I do not have these speaking dilemmas, I nevertheless identify with his sense of insufficiency to do the important work of preaching the good news to the least of these.

Motive: Why should we preach?

We should preach because we have been called to do so and persuaded that this is the way that God would have us make the biggest difference in this world. This calling is not just a call to stand and recite the words of scripture but a call to interpret that scripture for the present age. We should preach because we have tasted of the liberty that is in Christ and should share God's disdain for bondage. Like David Walker, our actions should signal our support for the notion that while we are free we are dissatisfied because others still struggle in bondage.[22] We preach as voices crying in the wilderness aiming to prepare the way for the Lord to save both spiritually and holistically but we must be careful that the former form of salvation is not neglected. The reason for this is that according to H. Richard Niebuhr Jesus was not simply a social prophet but he was concerned about spiritual oppression and this information was inferred when Niebuhr wrote that Jesus' "mission can never be forced into the pattern of an emancipator from merely human oppressions."[23] At the same time people would be hard-pressed to have faith in eternal rewards of spiritual salvation without experiencing the tangible evidence of salvation and liberation on this side of eternity.

The preacher should preach with both proactive and reactive aims. The preacher should proclaim the gospel in order to prevent bondage from becoming more of an issue in our communities by informing the hearers of the traps that exist. For example, preacher should preach against sexual immorality not just to prevent God's wrath but also to prevent the social issues that result from such activity including teenage pregnancy and escalating rates of AIDS and other sexually transmitted diseases. But the preacher's ministry should also be reactive and therefore prophetically respond to the bondage that already exists in our society. There are people who are in bondage who want to be able to leave the church with a sense of hope that God is working on their behalf and part of ensuring this is to deal with specific moral evils that persons experience. The preacher has limited power to affect everyone's situation individually; but the preacher is able to point every hearer to the God who is not limited. We should preach because we understand that God is the liberator.[24] "God liberates us totally and holistically" and this means that God has emancipated us from "bondage, both spiritual and material."[25]

We should also preach because, in the words of Theodore Walker Jr., to fail to work for the achievement of both freedom and empowerment "counts as a failure to serve God."[26] We must be careful that as preachers we do not preach for self-serving aims. This reminds me of the prosperity gospel preacher who is seemingly most often found in mega-churches who claim to preach liberation but really offer false hope. These persons who have become rich while pushing this doctrine should be asked the question "How can you preach prosperity and have a huge mega-church, but around your mega-church you have poor folk who are not benefiting from the prosperity in your message?"[27] Hearkening back to the issue of self-awareness the preacher must be sober to ensure that his or her motives are not impure and also to prevent the liberated preacher from becoming an oppressor.

The church cannot be a place of bondage led by the preacher as the principal oppressor. Church history is filled with examples of liberated persons becoming oppressors especially when the persecution of the Christian church turned inward during periods like those under Constantine. Persons fled Europe to this country in order to have religious freedom but then sought to bind persons to their doctrine after these oppressors became liberated. I contend that just as oppressive behavior is learned so are the expectations of liberation. So we must preach partly in order to proclaim the liberty we practice and enjoy. Ultimately our motivation for preaching the gospel must be born out of our love of God and neighbor in support of the purpose of the church and its ministry that is to increase this twofold love among people.[28] Augustine once wrote that one does not understand scripture, of which the gospel is a part, if his or her understanding of scripture does not interpret scripture to build this "double love of God and neighbor."[29]

Method: How should we preach?

The preacher must preach in a way that raises the issues concerning humankind and then provides hope for the waiting congregation through a hermeneutic that portrays God as the principle force of liberation. In other words, the preacher should communicate the truth in a way that juxtaposes the reality of the congregation with the ideal as interpreted from scripture. In my experience, there are at least two models that inform how a preacher concerned with the holistic liberation of people may use to engender hope in the sermon's hearers.

The first model is the correlation model of preaching as introduced or termed by Paul Tillich.[30] This model is helpful because it uses an organizational observation to create tension between what humanity experiences periodically and the hope for a God-directed resolution. It correlates a specific text with the common experiences of the congregation so that the hearers will be able to find hope in that particular passage of scripture. For example, I preached a sermon entitled "Hope for a Deteriorated Existence" based on the text of Luke 7:11-17. The condition of existence reflected in the text is that this woman's existence had deteriorated. My organizing observation was the following:

There are times in life where things go from bad to worse; when such conditions prevail, God is near enough to comfort us and His power can and will turn things around.

This observation connected with the audience who was familiar with the experience of things in live going from bad to worse and showed that in this text God responds to our reality in an effort to either correct or improve our situation. This model for preaching is effective for communicating truth connected to my theology because it confronts the bondage that persons face and offers God's alternative.

The second model is the dialectic model as derived from G.W.F. Hegel.[31] Similarly to the correlation method, this method juxtaposes the real with the ideal or the antithesis with the thesis in an effort to inspire persons with the good news that it is possible to transition from the real to the ideal. In particular, the antithesis recounts the negative reality that exists in contradistinction to the ideal found in a selected passage of scripture.[32] In the antithesis, the preacher can address the conditions "that must be altered" and expose the issues that await God's corrective action.[33] To isolate the antithesis in our society we should ask questions such as "where is the good news in the text?" and "where is God in the text" because only then can we convincingly make the case that our message is worth hearing.[34] This homiletical method is helpful in preaching for the holistic liberation of persons because it may be used to highlight the social issues that contradict the character of God.

Message: What Should We Preach?

As we discussed earlier, one of the foundational elements of preaching is truth and above all else preachers are called to tell the truth. This means first and foremost the preacher must be able to preach the truth found in the Biblical text and the preacher is called to "reprove, rebuke, exhort" understanding that doing so may make people uncomfortable.[35] In other words, the preacher must preach the gospel which cuts by design and is able to confront the oppressor in each of us. It has been said that Christian preaching must focus on Jesus because "At the heart of Christian preaching there must be a theological substratum of Jesus Christ" and because "Jesus is able to meet the fundamental needs of humanity.[36] I agree and add to this that we should preach Christ and Him crucified for spiritual salvation but also as the unparalleled example of how in God no bondage is too burdensome. We should stress elements of the Christus Victor theory of atonement. This theory stresses Jesus' defeat of the devil as he escaped the bondage of death.[37] This should be preached because it provides a picture of how the power of God makes the impossible possible and makes escaping bondage a feasible goal.

Not only should we preach Jesus' death, burial, resurrection and ascension but we should also preach about the ministry of Christ. We need to preach about Jesus to affect liberation because as James Hopkins once wrote that in Jesus' proclamation in Luke 4:18-19 Jesus showed that His mission was to be "the anointed liberation Spirit with us."[38] If we would be called Christian or "Christ-like" we should reflect the ministry of Jesus. The preacher should be an extension of the ministry of Jesus who was never simply concerned with the spiritual part of man. It can be argued that Jesus never distinguished between the body and the spirit as if one part should be nurtured while the other is neglected.

Jesus not only addressed sin but persons' conditions of existence such as the blind, deaf, and the lame.[39] Jesus exemplified the principle that God cares and this is what Christian preaching targeting the liberation of persons should proclaim. This is only right if we are to believe Howard Thurman who wrote in reference to Jesus that "Christianity as it was born in the mind of this Jewish teacher and thinker appears as a technique of survival for the oppressed."[40]

To accomplish this preaching must be a corrective for human consciousness and confront the causes of the conditions of bondage.[41] It is true that the preacher who wishes to engage in transformative preaching needs to preach messages that "address sin and oppression wherever it is found whether in societal structures or in the consciousness of individuals."[42] Jesus always told the truth about the issues that existed and did not hold his peace in order to keep the peace. We as preachers cannot afford to participate in what Earl Ofari Hutchinson referred to as the "shameful silence of too many black ministers" who along with membership were silent as more persons fell into bondage through the removal of social programs designed to help our people.[43] For example, one of the more pervasive issues in our community is poverty and therefore it is a subject that must be broached from the pulpit. In this regard I agree that "We must not just preach to the poor but must preach about the poor."[44]

The aim of this work has been to present my theology for preaching as a product of my personal development and my overall understanding of God. I am fully aware of the fact that this is not an end to the conversation and that my personal maturation and evolution will yield changes to this theology. At least for the moment, as a preacher this is where I stand.

Christology

The final paper in this chapter focusing on theology is my final paper for my Christology course. This is one of the works of which I am most proud because of the accolades that I received for its depth of argument. The assignment description listed the requirements for each paper submission and each paper had to cover certain subjects. The paper not only had to discuss the ontology of Christ (human and divine), but also how we believed that Jesus accomplished the atonement among other things. Over the years, my Christology has remained the same with me not possessing either a high or a low Christology but a Christology somewhere in the middle. Similarly, to the previous paper, how one sees Christ influences one's teaching and preaching on the subject as well as one's theology. My hope is that this work inspires others to wrestle with their own theology about Christ. My Christology paper is below.

Introduction

The aim of this paper is to present a personal Christology that has been shaped by several factors. I will begin by defining Christology before proceeding to discussing the two theological issues that must be addressed in any valid Christology. Following this, I will discuss both the ontology of Jesus and the soteriology that surrounds Jesus. The former will address the nature or being of Jesus while the latter will discuss four prevailing theories of how Jesus atoned for humankind. I will then take the steps of comparing my own beliefs regarding revelation, salvation and the normative nature of Christ to the corresponding beliefs of four major traditions. In the end, the hope is to make clear where I stand concerning my Christology.

Definition of Christology

Christology is the study of who Jesus is and who Jesus was and it is also the study of what Jesus did and what Jesus yet does. In other words, Christology addresses both the past and present identity of Jesus while also tackling the past and present activity of Jesus. In this there is the dichotomy between the historical Jesus and the Christ of faith. The former describes the person of history whose existence is verified and noted in extra-biblical sources such as the writings of Josephus and others.[45] It includes what can be proven regarding Jesus' identity and activity while on this earth. The latter describes that which Christians maintain and believe about Jesus without extra-biblical and other forms of support such as archaeological evidence. Historical records testify to the fact that Jesus of Nazareth was a living human being before he died but his followers proclaimed that Jesus rose from the dead. When discussing the Christ of faith, one also has to discuss what one believes regarding the continual presence of Christ among his disciples even unto the present age. This cannot take place within a vacuum but must also address what one believes about the Christ's present identity.

Two Theological Problems: Historical and Experiential

These two problems are issues that must be dealt with in any Christology because they are concepts with which each believer in Christ must wrestle. The historical problem deals with the amount of verifiable historical evidence that is necessary for one to believe that Jesus is the Christ of faith who died and was raised from the dead.[46] Another way of stating this problem is that each believer must determine for himself or herself how much evidence he or she needs regarding the historical Jesus in order to believe in and commit to the Christ of faith. I must confess that when it comes to my personal wrestling with this issue I need to have some empirical evidence. It matters to me that there are witnesses to Jesus' existence other than the biased accounts of his followers found in the biblical text. While I esteem the bible and it is authoritative for my life, I need to be able to have confidence that I am not just a disciple of the imaginary. The fact that other sources say that

Jesus lived and died is enough for me in wrestling with this problem. Regardless of the fact that I came to know the gospel before asking such questions about the historical Jesus, now that I am a person of intellect and have to answer questions from those outside of the faith. The proof that exists which supports the life and death of Jesus is sufficient for me to place my faith in him as my Savior and Lord.

The second problem that must be addressed in any valuable Christology is that of the experiential issue. This issue deals with how Jesus is experienced within the community of faith and this includes the continual presence of Jesus with humankind. In other words, answering this question involves covering that which one believes about Jesus continual presence and influence after his death. I believe in the resurrection of Jesus Christ and this is part of the way that Jesus' influence persisted even after his death. His influence was further seen in the ministries of those who followed him especially in the apostles. The cataclysmic transformation evident in Jesus' apostles, who were shaky before Jesus' death but bold and confident after his reported resurrection, served as evidence that they believed in Jesus' persistent and continual presence. One of the things that separate Christianity from other religions is the belief that belief is insufficient but that one must have some type of experiential encounter with Christ. This means that at some point the gospel had or has to come alive in the minds and hearts of its hearers at which Jesus becomes resurrected in them. At that moment when the gospel is accepted sincerely I believe that one experiences Christ including receiving the Holy Spirit which at times has been called the Spirit of Christ. For every believer there is a time or perhaps an event where it all becomes real for the believer.

At that moment the Holy Spirit makes us new creations and we are born again. The ultimate evidence of this experiential encounter with Jesus is the transformed life and the continual reflection of Christ in one's daily life. In other words, the convincing proof that one has had an encounter with Jesus is the fact that one is focused on extending Jesus' ministry now that he has ascended. After an authentic experience with Christ one is no longer the same and cannot simply return to his or her former condition of existence. For me I knew that I had been changed as my outlooks on both life and death changed. This change was coupled with the fact that my intentions and behavior began to change including my gradual decline in the use of profanity. Only after Jesus was raised in me did I experience the overwhelming joy I had only heard other believers talk about.

Ontology

I must now transition to discussing Jesus' ontology or his actual being. Jesus has always been the eternal Second Person of the Trinity and always existed with God. Being part of the Trinity meant that from eternity Jesus shared the same substance as God and the Holy Spirit. I am not sure of Jesus' physical state prior to the incarnation but I am convinced of Jesus pre-existence. My Christology is partially a kenotic Christology where I believe Jesus emptied of himself and condescended to humankind and became human. In doing this, Jesus voluntarily gave up his eternal privileges and became subject to God in order to make the atonement for humankind. In becoming human, Jesus became the incarnate Logos or the enfleshed eternal purpose of God that was to save humankind.[47] The incarnation is the climax of other events that reflected the embodiment of the Logos since creation.[48] In order to effect humankind's salvation, Jesus became completely human with all of humanity's limitations.[49]

This includes the facts that Jesus transitioned from having all power to having some power, from knowing all to having limited knowledge, and perhaps from being everywhere to being at one place at each particular time. To this end, since the gospels are an interpretation themselves, I judge the portrayal of Jesus in Mark of having all power (over creation, supernatural, human illness and death) to be a theological construct rather than historical reality.[50] I do believe Jesus had power and that Jesus had prophetic knowledge due to his relationship with the Father but that does not make him all powerful or all knowing. However

I disagree with Thomas Aquinas who believed that at conception Jesus had the full knowledge of God and of his relation to God.[51] It explains his struggle in Gethsemane. If Jesus knew all including the specifics about what he would experience one must wonder why he asks God for an explanation regarding God forsaking him.[52] I agree with John Macquarrie's comparison of Jesus with Dr. King where both knew the risks of their ministries but nonetheless traveled to places where danger lurked.[53] The story of Lazarus is a great testimony to the fact that Jesus could not occupy more than one locale at a time judging from Mary and Martha's comments.[54] In this model of ontology, Jesus walked like we walk only he served God completely and his higher form of humanity is why the bible could say that he grew in favor with God and man.[55] Even in his humanity, Jesus endeavored to do the will of God to whom he made himself subject. For me, to think of Jesus as being equal to God while a baby or to think of Jesus as having only human existence and none before his birth seems too extreme. Neither pole makes much sense but, as I have shown, it is possible to see Jesus as having two distinct states of existence.

With regard to his nature, I also believe that Jesus while on earth was divine. This divinity does not denote equality with God while on earth but means to communicate that Jesus was like God or reflected God's character. This is why Jesus could say that whoever had seen him had seen the invisible God because he was demonstrating the character of God by living a life consistent with God's terms and God's will.[56] What made Jesus' humanity a higher form of humanity was not some extra help that he possessed or the mythical virgin conception and birth but rather that Jesus was the human being that God always wanted. He showed us what it takes to please God in the lives that we live. I believe that Jesus' humanity helps us to see that he did not have any more help in living a righteous life than we have. It all came down to the choices that he made. Therefore just as Jesus embodied the Logos or thought of God, so we also may embody or live out the purposes for which we were made because we too at one point were in the mind of God before we came forth.⁵⁷ Since Christology deals with who Jesus was and is, and while this first portion has dealt with the former, I must also address who I believe Jesus to be at this moment. Jesus is our high priest and the mediator of the New Covenant. Jesus has reassumed his position in glory and has required all that he gave up to win our salvation.

Soteriology

Soteriology is the study of how Jesus accomplished our salvation or atonement. There are four main theories of how exactly Jesus accomplished the atonement for humankind and they include the satisfaction theory, the Christus Victor theory, the ransom theory, and the moral exemplar theory. Each of these theories will be discussed and care will be given to articulate the elements of each theory with which I agree or disagree.

To begin, the satisfaction theory of atonement, traditionally associated with Anselm of Canterbury, has several different explanations.⁵⁸ The main crux of this theory is that Jesus had to die in order to satisfy God in order to prevent God's wrath from being poured out on humankind. In this model, Christ becomes our substitute and our salvation is purchased through the death of Christ and humankind is saved from God.⁵⁹ Jesus' death satisfies the "offended honor of God."⁶⁰ It is the means by which humankind is able to be forgiven.⁶¹ I agree with the concept that Jesus' death purchased a pardon for humankind and saved mankind from damnation. However, I do not agree with the portrayal of God as the problem because sinful humankind became problematic and evoked God's wrath.

The Christus Victor theory of atonement is one that portrays Jesus as having been the key piece in God's game of chess with the devil. The centerpiece or focus of this theory is that Jesus accomplished our atonement by helping God become victorious over Satan through the death and resurrection of Jesus.⁶² This model suggests that the way that Jesus accomplished our atonement was by dying and being raised he overcame all evil forces. In other words, through his death and resurrection Jesus has triumphed over the devil and has become ruler over all; both the demonic and the evil that resides in each of us. In this theory, humankind is saved from the devil and from ourselves.[63] With regard to this theory, I agree that Jesus' death and resurrection has caused him to triumph over the devil and he is qualified to reign over all. I also agree that we are saved from ourselves because Jesus has power over it all and through him victory over all evil is possible.

The ransom theory describes the concept that humankind was kidnapped by Satan and that God had to do something in order to purchase humankind's freedom or pay the ransom to Satan who held sinners captive.[64] In this model, humankind is saved from the devil and Jesus' death is not a form of deception but rather a payment to Satan for our freedom. I agree that a kidnapping of sorts has taken place ever since sin has pervaded human existence but I strongly disagree that the devil needed to be paid by God in order for us to be free. According to this theory, Jesus was a perfect man who did not deserve death and so when the devil, who had the power of death, claimed Jesus in death the devil overstepped his bounds and therefore forfeited everything. In other words, according to this model God tricked the devil. In this model, humankind was saved from the devil and our atonement was accomplished through the death of Jesus.[65] It is our duty to then to attach ourselves to Christ through faith and baptism in order to gain freedom.[66] While I agree that the death of Jesus was integral, I have a problem with a portrayal of God who does not have all power and who has to mirror Satan's deceitful activity in order to defeat Satan. While I'm comfortable with notion of the condescension of God to humankind, I am not comfortable with the image of God condescending to Satan's level. This model, a variant of the Christus Victor model, also in my view diminishes God by insinuating God's subservience to Satan in a sense. It does not make sense that an all-powerful God would have ceded control of humankind to Satan. I agree however that humankind was of such value to God that God was willing to pay the ultimate price in order to purchase our redemption with Sin being the slave master rather than Satan.

The moral exemplar theory states that humankind's atonement was accomplished through the perfect moral example found in the loving death of Jesus.[67] In this model, Jesus died and therefore demonstrated unselfishness, true sacrifice and the sacrificial love of God according to patristic writers such as Augustine of Hippo.[68] Peter Abelard is another person who was linked with this claim that atonement is accomplished through "a change within human being."[69] The emphasis of this theory is on the "unconditional nature and transforming power of God's love."[70] Jesus demonstrated the sacrificial love that we are called to mimic if we would be found pleasing to God. We gain our atonement through this ultimate pattern of selflessness that leads one to serve others. The enemy in this theory is not the devil or God but it is ourselves.[71] In this model Jesus came to save us from ourselves by showing us what God desired from humankind when God first created humankind. Jesus accomplished our atonement by being an example that if followed would lead one to living a life pleasing to God. I concur with the notion that ultimately we need to be saved from ourselves but I disagree with the premise that following Jesus' example is sufficient for salvation because it does not address our sinful condition of existence. In my view, it is possible for this model to descend into a sort of works righteousness that covers or masks sin but fails to adequately address sin. At the same time, I believe that the sign of one's atonement is more than an audible confession to that effect but that it must include a lifestyle that effuses commitment to God.

Comparing Other Traditions

This final section addresses four faith traditions and answers the question of how each of these traditions sees salvation, revelation and the normative nature of Jesus. In other words, it discusses how we are saved, how God is revealed, and whether or not Jesus is the measure of truth in these other traditions. I will also locate my own Christology within the views of these various traditions and indicate the components with which I agree and disagree. These traditions include the evangelical tradition, the mainline protestant tradition, the catholic tradition and the theocentric tradition.

The evangelical tradition was born out of the fundamentalists who take a fundamental and very literal approach to the interpretation of scripture.[72] In this tradition, salvation is only possible in Christ.[73] This salvation is not by works but only through faith.[74] As a result, much of the energy expended by evangelicals is in attempting to convert others. The evangelical tradition softened on some of the hardline stances taken by the fundamentalists including the respect for science and ecumenical dialogue. But even this dialogue was designed in order to learn other faiths to the extent that converting members of these other faiths would be easier or more feasible. This tradition conservatively views the Bible and Jesus as God's only sources of revelation and believes that God is not revealed through nature or through other religions or traditions.[75] In this tradition, Jesus is absolutely normative or the ultimate measure of truth within this tradition.

In the mainline protestant tradition salvation is also through Jesus Christ as it is believed with those who practice the evangelical tradition.[76] According to the protestant model the followers of other religions seem to attempt to "effect their own salvation" or "force God's hand."[77] At its core, the mainline protestant tradition relies on both an ontological component as well as an epistemological component. In other words, the being of humankind or its sinful condition necessitates salvation while salvation is only mediated through the word as the only sufficient means to bring understanding.[78] However, this tradition differs from the evangelical tradition with regard to revelation. This tradition posits that no one can truly know God outside of Jesus Christ which is why other revelation is helpful it is not sufficient to save. This tradition believes that there is revelation outside of the Bible and outside of our particular faith. This particular revelation is termed as by Emil Brunner as "creation revelation" and by Paul Tillich as "general revelation" but this differs from "natural revelation" because it is not something that humankind discovers but something that God reveals.[79] To Paul Knitter, this revelation is rooted in the teachings of the New Testament where God is revealed to the Gentiles.[80] In this tradition Jesus is the ultimate revelation of God and therefore normative and the standard by which all other claims of truth are measured.

The catholic model is distinguished from the previous two models discussed in that it agrees with them on one point while disagreeing with them on others. It agrees with the others on the premise that Jesus is normative.[81] This tradition accepts that since Jesus made the atonement for humankind salvation is indeed possible outside of Christianity. In other words, the redemptive work has already been accomplished and so any religion that leads persons to live lives that would align with Jesus' example is effective in securing persons salvation. The catholic tradition holds that the church is a sign or sacrament of this salvation. This model also holds that not only is salvation available beyond the parameters of the Christian religion but so also is revelation attainable outside of the "borders of Christianity."[82]

The theocentric model states that Jesus does not have to be normative.[83] While Jesus remains normative for Christians, in this model Christians are able to refrain from insisting that Jesus be normative for others.[84] I disagree with the theocentric model on this very point. At the same time, in this model revelation is possible because in rejecting the incarnation, this model calls for God to be encountered in Jesus as well as other persons.[85] This model makes God the center rather than Jesus or even the church.[86] Although not explicitly mentioned, Knitter paints this model as one in which Jesus is not the only way to salvation. I agree that God is revealed in others beside Christ; but I hold that Jesus is the unparalleled revelation. Further I disagree with this model on the point of Jesus being the only way to salvation.

I agree with evangelicalism and mainline Protestantism that salvation is found in Christ but I cannot be sure of how this is accomplished in the sense that I believe that there are people whose atonement has been purchased but who will never hear the name of Jesus. I am confident in the path that I have chosen but I cannot in good conscience condemn anyone because I know that only God can distinguish between the wheat and the chaff. In my Christology, mainline Protestantism is correct that salvation is in response to the human condition and that one has to hear the gospel in order to receive the gospel and respond through faith. I agree that the Bible is a source of revelation; but I cannot limit the scope of God's revelation to a canon created by flawed individuals. I do believe in revelation from Creation where God has made it so that the heavens declare the glory of God and that creation testifies to the premise that there is someone greater than us who created it all. If one defines revelation is the truth of God being revealed, then I cannot confidently say that other faith traditions do not have truthful elements.

Ultimately, I find that my Christology falls between the mainline protestant tradition and the catholic tradition. This is because I agree with the traditions where they concur on the ideas that Jesus is normative; and that revelation is possible outside of Christianity but with regard to salvation being only possible in Christ I am not sure. None of the traditions allow for what is possible because each tradition takes a stand on each of the questions at hand including the question of soteriology. To be honest, I feel that God is the only one able to determine if salvation is attainable outside of Christ and to assume otherwise is to usurp God's authority as the ultimate judge. I believe that mainline Protestantism is too conservative; and that Catholicism is too liberal in this regard. Therefore, I am not sure if salvation is attainable through other faith traditions and through a medium who is not Jesus. However, I would have to lean in the direction of the more liberal view that would answer this question with a "maybe" as opposed to a "probably not." In other words, I cannot in good conscience believe that persons who are isolated from the rest of civilization are automatically doomed because they have not heard the gospel. I would like to believe that as long as these persons without access to the gospel accept the revelation of God communicated through creation as evidence of God's existence that this may be considered as enough for God to save them. In this view, it maybe that Jesus' atoning sacrifice is effective for all as postulated by the catholic model, but I cannot be certain. However, if I had to choose only one of these positions I could only choose the negative with regard to salvation apart from Christianity because while other avenues are possible, I am only convinced of the one way who is Jesus.

Conclusion

To summarize, my Christology developed and presented in this work reflect the willful engagement of the issues that need to be addressed and the questions that must be answered by any Christology. I have stated that the confirmed existence or life and death of Jesus on this earth are significant and necessary in order for me to follow the Christ of faith. Furthermore, I have described how Jesus is yet experienced on this earth especially in the lives of Christian believers. Care has been given toward addressing the ontology of Jesus that best represents my beliefs consistent with my formative factors. I was also able to take a stand regarding soteriology and found that my personal views on the subject constitute a mix of the four theories of atonement that I described. Lastly, I compared the views on revelation, salvation and the normative nature of Christ found in four different traditions and located my own views as between that of mainline Protestantism and Catholicism. This exercise has been helpful but I realize that as I continue on my Christology will likely evolve. Each person must take the time to rewrite or tweak his or her Christology as more study and experience will no doubt further shape what we believe concerning Christ.

---

[1] McGrath.

[2] Thomas, 19.
[3] Harris, *The Word Made Plain*, 38.
[4] Harris, *The Word Made Plain*, 38.
[5] LaRue, *The Heart of Black Preaching*, 115.
[6] Sanders, *Empowerment Ethics for a Liberated People*, 116.
[7] Evans, 131.
[8] LaRue, *Power in the Pulpit*, 121.
[9] Franklin, 2.
[10] Augustine, 164.
[11] Sanders, "Preaching for Advocacy through Love"
[12] Proctor, 5.
[13] Carter, "Who Am I as Preacher?"
[14] John 8:36
[15] LaRue, *Power in the Pulpit*, 7.
[16] LaRue, "How to Get Better at the Foolishness of Preaching Part II"
[17] Harris, *The Word Made Plain*, 1.
[18] Braxton, "Sanctification for Proclamation, Walking with God"
[19] LaRue, *Power in the Pulpit*, 154.
[20] Thomas, 29.
[21] LaRue, *Power in the Pulpit*, 13.
[22] C.f. Hopkins, 224.
[23] Niebuhr, *Christ & Culture*, 110.
[24] Harris, *Preaching Liberation*, 24.
[25] Hopkins, 160.
[26] Sanders, *Empowerment Ethics for a Liberated People*, 117.
[27] Haynes, 23.
[28] Niebuhr, *The Purpose of the Church and Its Ministry*, 27.
[29] Augustine, 30.
[30] Harris, *The Word Made Plain*, 38.
[31] Harris, *Preaching Liberation*, 99.
[32] Ibid., 100.
[33] Proctor, 28.
[34] LaRue, *I Believe I'll Testify*, 104.
[35] Hicks, 17.
[36] Carter, "What Am I Preaching?"
[37] McGrath or Weaver
[38] Hopkins, 194.

[39] LaRue, *The Heart of Black Preaching*, 227.
[40] Thurman, 29.
[41] Harris, *Preaching Liberation*, 9.
[42] Ibid., viii.
[43] Franklin, 132.
[44] Sanders, "Preaching for Advocacy through Love"
[45] Macquarrie, 349.
[46] C.f. Macquarrie, 348.
[47] Macquarrie, 375.
[48] Ibid., 392.
[49] Guthrie, 239.
[50] C.f. Mark 4:35-5:43.
[51] Macquarrie, 354.
[52] Mark, 15:43
[53] Macquarrie, 357.
[54] C.f. John 11:21, 32.
[55] Macquarrie, 359.
[56] C.f. John 6:46
[57] C.f. John 1:1-14.
[58] McGrath, 326.
[59] Weaver, 19.
[60] Ibid., 17.
[61] McGrath, 326.
[62] McGrath, 322.
[63] Weaver, 19.
[64] Ibid., 16.
[65] Ibid., 19.
[66] Musser and Price, 45.
[67] Weaver, 19.
[68] McGrath, 331.
[69] Musser and Price, 46.
[70] Migliore, 185.
[71] Weaver, 19.
[72] Knitter, 76.
[73] Ibid., 85.
[74] Ibid., 87.
[75] C.f. Ibid., 76.
[76] Ibid., 104.
[77] Ibid., 102.

[78] C.f. Ibid., 104-106.
[79] Ibid., 97.
[80] Ibid.
[81] Knitter, 133.
[82] Ibid., 140.
[83] Ibid., 149.
[84] Ibid., 152.
[85] Ibid., 153.
[86] Ibid., 166.

5

Reflective

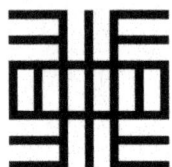

Much of our time spent in seminary revolved around reflecting upon our theologies, our ministries and the works of others. As mentioned previously, in a practical sense, teachers called upon students to reflect and then offer critique on presentations as well, as sermons give during class time. This tendency to get us to focus on our feelings and thoughts by looking back over experiences taught us to be more in tune with our feelings. It did not serve us sufficiently, for our professors, to simply experience things and then not to engage intellectually and come to some conclusion about its worth or impact on each of us. While this book includes no particular work from my time in my Christian Ethics class, that class defined different types of morality, and forced us to reflect on ethical dilemmas including ethical parenting (including if it is more ethical to allow same-gender loving couples to adopt or to allow children to languish in foster care). Students participated in groups that presented on different ethical subjects such as the DSK Affair, Steve Bartman, prosperity preaching, domestic violence, the death penalty, business ethics, and abortion. Students also participated in class discussions. This class exposed that many issues, while we would like to see them as black and white are actually shades of gray.

For the purposes of this chapter, four reflections exist that I chose to include. An analysis of one of my first Hampton University Ministers Conference experience served as the basis for an experiential learning credit as I offered reflection an analysis of the materials and messages presented during that conference. The second work came as the result of my experience in a pastoral care class, which required that each student reflect on one moment in ministry. The third is a reflection from my time spent at the REM Pastoral Care Conference held in Richmond, Virginia in February 2011. The final category of reflections could have perhaps been included as part of the chapter on textual works as each of them deal with preaching in a sense. These latter reflections include reflections on three works important for our class.

Hampton

This chapter begins with a reflection of one of several of my trips to "Our Home by the Sea." From the first time that I attended one of the Hampton University Ministers Conference sessions, I was determined to try and never miss another. It was my first experience with any preaching conference and to say that it impacted me would be an understatement. Each time I go to Hampton, I am reminded of what preaching is supposed to look like and include. Each year inspires me to improve and step up my game as I hear some of the most effective preachers preach and as I hear lecturers like my second year preaching Professor, Dr. James Harris, lecture on the subject of preaching. The particular year for which I wrote this reflection called several impactful preachers to the campus. My analysis of this impactful session follows.

The 96th annual Hampton University Ministers Conference that convened from June 6 – 11, 2010 overall was a great experience and one that aided in my development in ministry. For the most part, the conference presenters were well chosen for both their academic prowess and their ability to discuss the theme for this year's conference: "Ministry and Integrity." Each year I look forward to the "Hampton Experience" because it has given me new insights in the past into how to perform relevant and effective ministry while also providing a relaxed atmosphere to fellowship and worship with others wrestling with the same call. Although the pace and schedule of events can feel overwhelming at times, this pace has precipitated me leaving the conference each year with my cup running over. This year's conference was no exception to this past precedent as it provided valuable tools and offered a time for reflection over my ministry and ways that I could improve. This paper seeks to provide a critical and constructive analysis of the experience. I will begin by discussing the first day of the conference that included the opening of the Choir Guild workshop as well as the opening worship service for the conference. Following this,

I will discuss the preaching and teaching that followed throughout the week in the order in which I experienced it all.

I traveled to the conference with my pastor and other associate ministers from my home church. We were uninformed as to the fact that the Choir Guild's opening would begin at 10:00am because this information was not received until after one had registered. Although the registration process went fairly smoothly, one of the things that should be changed is that people should be informed of the complete schedule before they register. As a result of our ignorance we arrived at the Choir Guild opening late and only heard the last ten to fifteen minutes of the opening sermon. The portions that we heard were informative and necessary as the speaker addressed the qualifications and preparation necessary for those who lead the congregation in worship. I felt that the direct instruction on praying and living with integrity were on-target with regard to being able to properly lead people in worship. The speaker rightly correlated integrity with trust and stated that if people are going to follow you, they first must be able to trust you. This helped me to remember to live my life above reproach not only as a minister but as a Christian so that I do not bring shame to God's kingdom and so that others have a reason to follow my leadership.

I felt that the speaker was also correct in stating that public worship should primarily be a reflection of private worship including in the life of the worship leader. This encouraged me to be more diligent in having time set aside for prayer, mediation and worship so that when God is ready to use me to lead in public, I would have been privately prepared. By using Isaiah 1 as the pericope, the preacher was able to lift up the idea of how we all need to surrender ourselves to God for God's exclusive use and how important self-examination is to the believer. The preacher told the truth and seemingly cared more about helping us along than getting people shouting and so it is encouraging to know that one's ministry can flourish even without compromising the gospel for Christian entertainment. One of the speaker's final exhortations resonates with me still and that is the admonition to stay out of gray areas in life in order to avoid the very appearance of evil so that my integrity is guarded and has no need to be questioned.

The opening worship of the conference itself was a very rewarding experience. The preacher's choir rendered arrangements of songs that I have never previously heard and may have been original arrangements. If so, this echoes the admonition of Dr. Willis Barnett who teaches his students that music ministries should strive to be original rather than simply singing mainstream songs. The fact that this particular church may practice this idea is encouraging and it lets me know that what Dr. Barnett suggests is not only possible but can be done extremely well. The preacher for the opening worship shared from the theme "Learning How to Live Beyond the Broken Pieces" and the text was Exodus 32:19 and 34:1. The overwhelming theme throughout this sermon is that we as leaders and preachers need to be like Moses in the sense of moving beyond the failures that we initiated and trust that God in God's mercy and grace will do some things over again. In my past there have been efforts that have failed because I like Moses became impatient and frustrated but I had to learn how to move on from those disappointments.

The speaker helped us to understand that to become consumed with failure leaves no room to seek God for greater success. I could relate to the later point that sometimes I have spent time in God's presence with a great expectation for what I was going to share with people and when I shared it they did not have any excitement. I have also felt at times that perhaps my ministry is not at a high demand like others my age because some people are fickle and grow weary with sound doctrine but want to be entertained. This sermon helped me to see that I could always use more patience and this characteristic is invaluable in ministry. One of the warnings given by the speaker that is useful to me is that I ought not to allow how people act to influence me to the extent that I lose my grip on what God has said. Perhaps one of the greatest moments of personal rejoicing came when the notion was raised in that Moses did not forfeit his ministry because of his failure and I thank God that all of my mistakes in the past did not cause me to forfeit the privilege of leading now. This point also sobers me so that I can try even harder to avoid the traps that are set for me.

The second day for me began with morning worship and after the morning song and other formalities the preacher stood and started to preach. The preacher's subject was "I'm Not Stuck, I Stayed" and the pericope was Acts 16:25-28 dealing with one of Paul and Silas' stints in prison where, after they prayed and sang, they and the other prisoners had an opportunity to leave but did not do so. One of the primary points shared by the preacher is that in John 17 Jesus prays for His disciples while they are in the world and does not pray for them to escape trouble but only for their endurance. I loved this point because much of what perpetrates as preaching tries to link the quality of your life with how good you have been without regard for the truth that trouble will come to all of us and some of it we will not be able to escape but only endure. Another helpful tidbit from the speaker was that as ministers of the gospel we do not need fans but friends who will tell us the truth at all costs instead of bowing at our feet.

Next the preacher shared that although the prisoners had a way of escape, they did not take it and the point is that not every open door is meant for us to walk through and not every open door is from God. This helps me in my context to wait on God before walking through any open door because not every opportunity available is an opportunity of which God wants me to take advantage. In discerning to stay put, Paul was in position to have his voice save the guard's life and protect that family's wellbeing. I have to be where God wants me to be so that I can be in position to let me voice be used by God in order for God to save somebody. Many preachers leave the places to which they have been assigned chasing packages, money and congregation sizes and leave churches without a voice and leave people with no hope. I firmly believe that if something is done God's way that it will never leave people without hope and this includes my belief that any condemnatory message without hope is not from God. Paul's voice gave the guard a reason to live in spite of what he saw and it is the preacher's responsibility to help people see hope even when what they see may leave them hopeless. In Paul's case, his integrity led to a life being saved because he was who he was supposed to be and where he was supposed to be and we should cease from calling ourselves Christians if we lack the integrity of trying to be like Christ.

The day continued with two lectures from people distinguished in academia. The first lecturer talked about integrity and how it means doing the right thing even when no one else is looking. This has been helpful to me as I have examined not only my public persona but also my private life in an effort to rid my life of habits that I would not want others to know about. I appreciated the reminder that in ministry we especially need to walk in integrity so that even if people never hear a sermon from us they will be able to discern a sermon based on our lifestyle. It helps in that regard to acknowledge the omnipresence of God who is there and examining our ways both in private and in public.

The second lecturer of the day discussed the critical question to be posed by every minister of the gospel: "What Am I Preaching?" The presenter suggested that the core of Christian preaching must be Christ; and this aids me in my endeavor to preach because Jesus is always relevant even though as Joel Gregory once said some preachers seem to be bored with Jesus. One of the teachers most effective illustrations was the picture of a dog walker who holds on to multiple dogs by their leashes to prevent them from mauling people and as preachers we are responsible for being led or walked by the gospel of Jesus Christ so our preaching does not end up mauling people. I agree wholeheartedly with the premise of the presenter that too often outside applications of the gospel become the focus of preaching instead of the God who makes these miracles possible. Jesus being the core of our preaching does not mean that this is all we should preach but rather the "Christ event" is the lens through which we can view the text so as to determine what we and others will see in the text.

In my attempt to be more prophetic, I agree further with the idea of the lecturer that what we preach should not fit in with this culture but should be distinctive because of the presence of Christ in our sermons.

Too much of what is called preaching fits in extremely well with our materialistic society and I am grateful for the reminder to keep my speech distinctive. The lecturer stated that we should preach Jesus because He is able to meet the fundamental needs of humanity as evidenced by the meeting of the principal need of humanity in salvation. Lastly, the teacher provided another excellent illustration in stating that just as a lifeguard is on duty while someone is being taught how to swim, we as preachers, although we are teaching others to swim, need to be mindful that in case we falter the Lifeguard is always present. The afternoon session concluded with the preached message "What is in Your Mouth?" taken from Proverbs 31:25-26. The message primarily focused on the need for integrity and holiness on the part of God's trumpets and that we as ministers should be focused on providing excellence in ministry even though in today's church incompetence has become the status quo.

At that evening's worship, the conference preacher shared a message from Jeremiah 1:1-10 entitled "A Prenatal Ordination." one could feel how the preachers immediately connected with this title since most preachers believe their ordination to be prenatal and that God knew us all before we were formed. The speaker accurately stated that the call of God comes to someone who has an identity, a particular family, a locality and amongst particular history. Even in my own call to ministry I can reflect and see that I did not come from a family of preachers or from a place that has produced many preachers but I have been called at a particular point in history for such a time as this and God called me to be who I am. The language behind the text suggests that the word for "knew" can be rendered "claimed" and so it is good news that God has claimed us as God's spokespersons even before we were formed. I was grateful for this reminder because it drove home the point that God is God and we are not.

The next point about how Jeremiah was sanctified or set at a distance encouraged me and served as a stern reminder to all of us that we should not try to be so close to the things or people from which God has set us apart. This does not mean that preachers are better than anyone but it would behoove preachers to behave as if they have been set apart. Next the preacher lifted the point that Jeremiah was consigned to a place and was not able to negotiate with God for his assignment and this lets me know that I should always be where I am assigned to be. The final major point that I took from the preacher's message is that in the text not just anybody or anything touched Jeremiah's lips. In that the preacher warned us all against allowing people other than God including other preachers or congregations to touch our lips and we should not touch our own lips. Preachers should not preach the creativity and work of others solely and should not preach simply what the congregation desires to hear and should not invent a message but should receive a sermon from God after personal study, prayer, and mediation.

The structure of the third day of the conference mirrored that of the second day with the exact same presenters. The morning preacher began the day with a message entitled "It Won't Happen Overnight" based in Genesis 22:9-18. The first issue that the preacher raised was with the preaching of today that is centered on gaining more possessions from God as if God is some type of cosmic Santa Clause who can be manipulated and conned. The preacher rightly stated that too much of preaching is focused on what you can get from God rather than what God can get from us. This preaching confuses God's favor with having more stuff and this is why many churches have left substance to become a circus. I have long voiced my opposition to this train of thinking that treats God as if God is a genie and one that answers to us instead of the other way around. I have always been skeptical of the claim that one can speak things into existence and this is supported by the scripture that talks about how God speaks those things which are not as though they were because God is the one who can call things into existence. This type of teaching that puts men in God's shoes seeks to make God our slave and this practice is prevalent in our churches where people think that God's only responsibility is to be at Christians' beck and call. It is this type of infantile thinking that the preacher dismissed as he declared that there are some assignments that you have to grow big enough to walk in.

The preacher drove this point home by using Abraham's story in the text and how in between his promise and the final product there were some tests including some that Abraham did not pass. The good news for me is that Abraham's failure in the tests did not prohibit God for still using Abraham to fulfill his assignment. It helps me to know, as someone who is looking to do greater ministry, that promotion according to the preacher is not based on perfection but on progress. The preacher stated that from the text we can know that assignments are tied to a place and once again I appreciated the reminder to stay where God has me until God assigns me to a different place. I agreed with the assessment in the message that as preachers specifically we need to be willing to trust God even amongst a lack of details even if the only instruction God gives is for us to stay where we are. Like Abraham we have to be willing to trust to the extent that we are able to worship God in spite of what we are carrying and then bless God not so much of what we gained but based on what God did not allow us to lose. Abraham reached the point of complete surrender and this point encouraged me to again make the conscious decision to completely surrender then and each day of my life to the will of God. As a result, this is the part of the sermon that resonated with me most because it led me to make a decision which according to Dr. Patricia Gould-Champ should be the goal of every sermon: to lead someone to make a decision.

Following the morning worship session, the first lecturer again rose to speak about integrity and the instructor's topic was "Integrity in Ministry in a Bulletproof Society." To help everyone understand the use of the bulletproof image the instructor had the staff play Raheem DeVaughn's song "Bulletproof" and this song lifted up some of the social issues that ministry ought to address if the church is yet going to have integrity in this society. I agree with the instructor that when it comes to institutional integrity part of that in the church deals with addressing social issues even those that are yet considered taboo in the

African American community. The presenter duly pointed out the fact that Jesus lived in a bulletproof society in which there were professional murderers and crime syndicates. This helped me to understand that like Jesus the church must have an edge about it so that it is not intimidated or afraid to do what's right even in the midst of all that is so wrong about our society. One of the most effective metaphors utilized by the instructor was the use of pottery that has been cracked after it has gone through the fire but the potters could use some type of corrective material to fill the cracks and sell the cracked vessel. The only way that the cracks could be seen or the corrective material's presence exposed is if the vessel was held up to the light. When the church is under scrutiny or held up to the light, the world should not see any cracks which symbolize the church's integrity.

This served as a good precursor to the speech by the U.S. Secretary of Education who lifted up the problem of education in this country. There is perhaps no greater social issue affecting the African American community today than the issue of education and it was encouraging to know that the executive branch of the federal government was interested in speaking to preachers who should also be community leaders about this community crisis. Part of the church having integrity is edifying the community especially in the area of education and providing resources for the community. The church has to be an advocate for children so that they can receive the education they need and deserve. The mission of the ministry of any church should include empowerment and education is one of the tried and true methods of empowering generations to succeed who can then reinvest in their communities of origin in order to help others succeed.

As the day continued, the second lecturer rose and began teaching from the subject "Why Am I Preaching?" The point of this lecture was to raise the importance of the preacher knowing who he or she is so that others are not allowed to define the preacher and create unbiblical and unrealistic expectations of the preacher. Using a pericope from the first chapter of the gospel of John, the teacher excellently pointed out how John called for a distinction to be made between the Savior and himself

– he said I am not Jesus. It was refreshing to hear a reminder from an academic and a pastor that we are not the Savior and it is not our job as preachers to meet every need but to provide a referral to the One who can supply every need. Each of us is unique because we have different experiences and different personalities and so the teacher exhorted us that while mentors are good each preacher has to be comfortable in his or her own skin. This makes the task of preaching a little easier knowing that I can be myself and still perform the road work of preaching in an authentic way. My individuality should not however set me above others in my own mind but like John I should see myself as part of a network of preachers who have a similar charge.

The lecturer noted that this model of John works for preachers today because not only is it biblical but what John did was audible. I agree with the preacher that part of the responsibility of each preacher is to sound the alarm like a rooster to wake others out of their deep sleep. I am grateful for the instructor's insistence that while titles are good; we as preachers all need to remember that fundamentally we are to function as a voice to reflect God's primary vehicle of revelation. Like John, preachers are vehicles that should carry what has been deposited in them, and we should be God's reporters of the greatest story ever told instead of making up news on our own. As the teacher rightly put it, God needs our voice more than God needs our brain. As musicians in orchestras perform a score that has been handed down to them and not of their own invention, we as preachers are held accountable for preaching the gospel that has survived in spite of all of us. If preachers are going to be ultimately effective, we need to live lives that reflect God's holiness and this was the main point of the noon speaker who preached "Reach Beyond the Veil" based in Matthew 26:6-13. The veil symbolizes separation from God and each other according to the preacher and we should not preclude others from seeing God's glory simply because we desire to be consumed with our wants and personal needs.

On this the third day, the next event was that of the Senior Statesman Hour and the preacher shared from the topic "The Danger of Continuing in Duty and Form" from Micah 6:6-8. The gist of this message was that preachers should not allow style, traditional practices, method or duty to become their master. In doing so the preacher falls into the trap of preaching to maintain relationships and continue having the same expectations rather than preaching for change. This day concluded with the sermon "RSVP" from the conference preacher who utilized Matthew 11:28-30 to lift up Jesus' invitation that can still be accepted after its initial acceptance. Oftentimes people try to push preachers into burnout, so it was refreshing to hear a preacher who works very hard to be honest about how spiritual life is able to weigh us all down. To that end, the recommendation of the preacher through the text was that whenever worship becomes a burden, we need to be sensitive and sensible enough to pull away and rest before exhaustion leaves us perpetually on edge. To further illustrate this point the speaker reminded those in attendance of how Jesus got some rest on the ship going across the Sea of Galilee while his disciples were busy worrying and succumbing to anxiety. If the disciples would have rested as Jesus did, they never would have noticed the storm. The final exhortation that blessed me was the notice that the yoke in the text can be compared to the oxygen tank in scuba diving: outside of the water, the tank is heavy but in the water it helps one to survive. I am thankful for this yoke that even while there is responsibility under this yoke, there is also freedom and a resource to help me survive even when ministry takes me into deep waters.

Due to illness I was unable to attend the Friday morning worship experience and so Thursday's exercises were the last activities in which I participated. The morning homiletician delivered a final stirring sermon entitled "I'm the One" rooted in the text of Luke 17:11-19 which discussed the miracle of the ten lepers where only one leper returned to give thanks to Jesus. Initially, the sermon allowed its hearers to engage in self-examination as the speaker duly noted that often times we ascribe value to people based on their condition and assign them a label that is

Reflective 185

designed to limit the labeled. The historical connection that the preacher made between these lepers and African Americans in history was excellent as he pointed out that in the text the lepers were called something that related to the condition of their skin that they could not hide or change. These lepers according to the speaker cried the same thing at the same time and this helps all of us in ministry to understand that we should not seek companionship with people who are satisfied with being in bondage. Unlike lepers, whatever we are dealing with should not be owned by us as permanent condition by calling attention to our condition and accepting the labels others may place on us. Like these lepers, most if not all of the miracles required action by someone other than God or Jesus in order for them to come to pass and so I agree with the preacher that people need to participate in their own miracles.

Before the second lecturer completed his three day journey, the first lecturer ended with a lecture entitled "Trafficking in Dangerous Memories" in which the importance and power of memories were highlighted. The second lecturer ended on the subject "What Am I Preaching" from the first chapter of the gospel of John. One of the major points of this teacher was that it is the job of the preacher to take people from being personal fans or fans of Jesus to followers of Jesus. One welcomed suggestion from the instructor was for every preacher to examine the motives of our toil and our motives will help us understand why we should be preaching. The goal of all preaching should be to bring someone to a decision to follow Jesus that much more sincerely and as a result our preaching to point to the Savior as the Lamb of God in a similar way that John pointed to Christ. The preacher pointedly stated that there is nothing wrong with appreciating the preacher; but the preacher should never receive the attention that the Savior deserves. One of the more sobering facts upon which the teacher expounded is that the grammar of the text tells us that John's ministry had an expiration date as will my ministry and so I need to [point why I am able. I have always believed the exhortation of the instructor that preachers should be invisible as much as possible in that I would rather people remember the gospel that I preach more than they remember my name. My structured experience with this year's conference ended with the sermon "Time to Make a Shift to a Different Kingdom" grounded in Romans 6:6-7 which again noted the importance of holiness and the need to keep fighting in the midst of our individual battles and struggles. I am grateful for all that I learned during this conference and I look forward to implementing some of the practical advice from the speakers and teachers. There is no place like Hampton.

Pastoral Care Reflection

Our pastoral care professor Harry Simmons, D.Min. taught us the value of reflecting on our ministry especially for the purpose of learning a lesson and improving as a result. A pastoral care practitioner must always be in the mood for self-evaluation to improve and be as impactful as possible. To that end, one of our assignments involved writing a reflection on an instance in our ministry where we faced some sort of difficulty or challenge and how it became resolved. The ministry even on which I reflected included a time where my pastor called upon me to teach Wednesday night Bible study in his absence. A reflection of this event follows.

Ministry Reflection Report

Information

The event on which I desire to reflect is a time when I was asked by my pastor to teach the corporate adult Wednesday night Bible Study class in his absence on a cold night in early March 2011. There were about twenty adults present for my lesson on "Context and the Fiery Furnace" where I intended to instruct them on the importance of keeping everything in context when doing biblical study. I used the text in Daniel 3 and after introducing the class to my philosophy of bible study, in that it should empower believers to study in a way that theologians study, I then used the principle of context to get them to question the traditional interpretation of this text where Jesus is interpreted to be present in the fiery furnace. The students were engaged and the looks on their faces throughout the lesson reflected deep thought and excitement as the result of learning something new. During the lesson, on a couple of occasions, persons questioned the context of other scriptures including the scripture that my pastor is using as a theme scripture for the year. Instead of answering these questions directly I found myself dodging the questions and sidestepping them in order to avoid answering.

Evaluation

As the result of my refusal to answer these difficult questions, the persons who asked the questions were disappointed but understanding. I was disappointed in myself and I questioned if I handled it in the correct manner. I wondered if I had failed in an attempt to balance my responsibility for informing the class and my duty to protect the reputation of my pastor who has not been seminary trained. I felt that in an effort to avoid betraying the trust of my pastor, who as the result of past experience is notably distrustful and paranoid at times, I had betrayed my duty as an instructor. Besides disappointment, I also experienced fear with regard to the prospect of my pastor learning that I had undermined his theology and this fear led me to back down from sharing some of my knowledge. As one who feels an eventual call to the pastoral ministry, I felt confused about how I should have handled the issue given the fact that I will have to eventually instruct ministers on my staff on how to handle similar instances. Besides these issues, my issues highlighted by this experience include how I can minister to the people while respecting the pastor as the theologian of the house so that I can avoid the appearance of evil and of an inflated ego. Part of me wanted to show the class how much I knew perhaps not to upstage my pastor but to increase their esteem of me and I felt impatient with dancing around the questions.

Analysis

Ministry to me is the practice of meeting the needs of the people through the various gifts that we all have been blessed with. With that said, what made this event ministry was the effort on the part of myself to utilize the teaching gifts to give persons clarity on scripture and the effort to empower them to be more independent. It was ministry because I used the opportunity to teach the students to think of studying the bible as an opportunity to learn more about the character of God while also learning about the persons that God expects us to be. These are the factors that made the experience positive while my own shortcomings due to fear previously explained made a portion of the experience negative. The factors at work that influenced the event included my pastor's trust issues, my pastor's trust of me teaching the class, and my increased knowledge as the result of my time at the School of Theology. At the same time, other factors that contributed to ho the event unfolded included the tendency for some persons in our church to run to our pastor every time it seems like someone has defied or undermined him. Lastly, my own struggle with not allowing confidence to devolve into arrogance influenced my life-long tendency to hold back knowledge so that I do not appear conceited. My options for a continuing ministering response in such a scenario include doing what I did or cowering to the pressure and external factors but another option is to remain faithful and true to the people and be honest with them about what I believe. Another option is perhaps choosing some type of middle ground where I give them as much as I can and on the questions or topics that could cause controversy simply refer them to the pastor for further clarification. I was limited in my ability to have enough wisdom to effectively navigate the tension between serving the people and serving the pastor who trusted me in his absence.

Theological Reflection

There are several theological issues within this ministering event. One of the principal theological issues is that of betrayal. While I would not put this experience on par with the betrayal of Jesus by Judas Iscariot, I believed that to show up my pastor would have been to throw him under the bus and to betray his trust which would have been especially egregious since he chose me to teach. Another theological concept is that of confusion, of which God is not the author, and part of the reason that I dodged the questions was to avoid the introduction of confusion where my pastor would be put in the position where he would have to discern if his associate ministry truly was attempting to sway the hearts of the people. In other words, I did not want what happened to Saul to happen to my pastor where after battle the people sang of how David killed tens of thousands while King Saul killed only thousands. I did not want this to feed into or reaffirm my pastor's distrust of persons in general. It is because I believe what the Bible says in that God appoints pastors after God's own heart and for me to do anything publicly to undermine that would be to disrespect and dishonor God. Further, an additional theological issue present in this ministry event is that of pride. While I believe pride in the form of self-esteem is appropriate and necessary, the Bible is clear that pride goes before the fall and that whoever exalts himself or herself will be humbled and in this case I did not want to pressure God to humble me so I humbly declined the opportunity to look more informed than my pastor.

Commitment

In light of the lessons learned through this ministerial context, while in the position of an associate minister I am committed to performing with excellence any assignments trusted to me by my pastor. However, I am also committed to taking a middle-ground approach and only share my knowledge publicly in the case that it will not obviously contradict the teachings of my pastor in order to minimize confusion until my pastor is able to trust persons more. This is because I am certain that I will experience something similar to this event and I am confident that I can serve both parties at the same time while avoiding the pitfalls of ego. Furthermore, in light of my foreseeable future in the pastoral context I commit to teaching those on my staff on how to handle this situation while also committing myself to do my due diligence in order to minimize occasions where for my ministers to speak the truth would be to contradict my teachings. I commit to being more honest with my pastor and sharing what I know with him for not only his benefit and that of the congregation, but also for the benefit of the entire kingdom.

REM Pastoral Care Conference Reflection

Dr. Simmons in our Introduction to Pastoral Care course offered participation in this conference as an alternative to taking the quizzes and final exam from the course based upon how the conference as designed would meet the desired class outcomes. The conference was a good experience with students staying at the host hotel and getting the opportunity to hear from the late great Dr. Katie Geneva Cannon and the great Dr. Jeremiah Wright, Jr. (with whom I took a picture). The fellowship at the conference was rich and rewarding. Below is my reflection.

Overall, the REM ACPE conference was a valuable experience. Part of what made it so enjoyable was being in the presence of my community or family of STVU students outside of the normal parameters of class. Another aspect of the conference that I appreciated was the forum to be able to discuss openly the divisive issue of race as it pertains to pastoral care. I appreciated being able to be given a snapshot view of the community of those persons that provide pastoral care. I will now reflect on the experiences under the teaching sessions of Dr. Katie Cannon, Dr. Irvin and Dr. Jeremiah Wright Jr. in a manner beginning with the conference opening with Dr. Cannon.

I had heard Dr. Cannon teach before at the Hampton Ministers Conference but she had discussed a different topic. Her approach has always been direct and unapologetic; and this instance was no different. She shot from the hip and did not mince words with regard to her topic. The second time that Dr. Cannon taught she talked about what to do when somebody tells you that your reality never happened. This line of teaching, especially utilizing hermeneutics from her own experience, resonated with me. It resonated with me because as people of faith we are encouraged to live our lives at times as if our conversion experience never happened.

Hearing Dr. Irvin discuss "transcendental whiteness" was surprising. I had never heard a white man so openly discuss the polarizing aspect of race and talk about how transcendental whiteness was fundamental to our society. It was interesting to hear from a white man that this air of superiority came over from Europe and became part of the very fabric of our society to the extent that the only way to completely eradicate it would be to start over. I really enjoyed the breakout sessions after the lesson in which other white persons expressed similar disgust with the pervasive white supremacy that is found in our society although these days it is more subtle than in the past. Both Dr. Cannon and Dr. Irvin are widely respected scholars and authorities on the subjects that they presented and so it was refreshing to hear such unmitigated truth from these persons. I was grateful for the REM conference being able to secure such qualified and distinguished contributors for our discussion on race.

The worship experience on that Thursday night was phenomenal. The dancers from the African Dance Company were exceptional and seemed authentic. I was grateful and humbled to be in the presence of such gifted persons and our community of faith. Dr. Kinney's message "My Eyes Have Seen the Glory" was inspirational and informative and helped me see the movement of the Spirit of God in different ways and not necessarily limited to the confines of my particular Christian faith. His hermeneutic of the boy with the bread saturated with cabbage steam still resonates with me as being a great example of what faith in God is like.

Dr. Jeremiah Wright did an excellent job staying within his assignment of lecturing instead of preaching at the banquet. The story of his colleagues going to meet the African descendants of tribes in the Amazon was compelling. The part that resonated with me most was when the chief asked Dr. Wright's colleagues that if they were still fighting the war against the white man why they were wearing his clothes. It is at this moment that I wondered to myself how much of ourselves people of African descent have lost while in this country to assimilation. It made me want to know more about these unknown stories.

The closing worship was a good old fashioned good time in church. Every part of the service including the singing of the Virginia Union University Choir was exceptional. Dr. Wright's sermon repeating the question of "Are we there yet" also was memorable. It made me remember that while progress has been made we still have far to go in order to achieve that perfect or complete community to which pastoral care is aimed to achieve. I am thankful to God for this experience and hope to learn through CPE unit(s) in the future.

Preaching Text Reflections

My second-year preaching course spent a great deal of time and effort on the task of reading and interpreting texts. To this end, we read *Interpretation Theory* by Paul Ricoeur, as well as *Metamorphosis & Other Stories*, *The Stranger*, and *A Lesson Before Dying*. However, as this was a preaching course, some of our reflections focused on works that dealt with the art and act of preaching. Two of the reflections upon which the course required us to write were of books written by our professor Dr. James Henry Harris including *Preaching Liberation* and *The Word Made Plain*. A third work, not necessarily classified as a text on preaching by some but nevertheless has merit, was Augustine's work *On Christian Doctrine*.

Preaching Liberation

The book *Preaching Liberation* was very helpful in raising the need for preaching to address the holistic liberation of persons to whom preachers preach. It caused me to reexamine the dialectic within concerning the honor and awesome responsibility of preaching. In other words when reminded of the great responsibility that I have it made me juxtapose this against the honor and privilege of having such a responsibility.[1] Ever since I was called to preach I have understood to a degree how I am responsible to God for what I assume to say on God's behalf. It was not until later however that I saw my responsibility not only to preach the gospel of the text but to bring good news to those who sit in all types of bondage. I was familiar with my responsibilities to reflect, study, and meditate in order to produce the best sermon I could but I did not have enough focus on giving people hope outside of the spiritual realm.[2] I was grateful for the reminder that as a preacher I should preach the liberating message of the gospel of Christ but I was also able to see that salvation in the spiritual realm while ignoring bondage in all others is problematic and insufficient.[3] Early on I understood the importance for me to be myself when preaching and to let my unique experience shine through. This was not to put myself on a pedestal but to be a transparent vehicle through which the hearers could be transported to a better reality for themselves knowing that I had practiced what I preached.

Another aspect of *Preaching Liberation* that stood out to me was the reminder of the preacher's dependence upon the Holy Spirit in order to have power in preaching. It was useful to read that ultimately regardless of all the efforts and hours put into study and hermeneutics, without the Holy Spirit the sermon has nowhere to go and to me is simply an eloquent religious speech.[4] Even after preaching for almost eight years I cannot help but be nervous when approaching the task of preaching and it is not due to a fear of flunking but rather due to an understanding that if God does not help me then the sermon cannot do any good.[5] The influence of the Holy Spirit is another reason why I believe that a sermon is never completely finished or perfect and that a preacher must be open to the move of the Spirit to make changes as the Spirit directs. The Holy Spirit is the wind in the preacher's sails that carries him or her forward and without the Holy Spirit the sermon is stationary and has no hope to empower anyone or stir anyone to action. I am thankful for the Holy Spirit's work and only seek to put myself in the position through study and other means so that the Holy Spirit has something to work with and is not depended upon to be the source of the complete "divination" of the sermon.

The Word Made Plain

One of the principle ideas that initially piqued my interest in *The Word Made Plain* was that concerning the interpretation of a text and "its context and presuppositions in written and unwritten form."[6] In particular I agreed with the sentiment that oftentimes people like to assume fixed interpretations for texts based on post-Enlightenment processes such as historical criticism. However, one of the things that fascinates me about preaching is how preachers can interpret texts differently using the variables within their own contexts and based on their own individual past experiences. Of course, as Dr. Harris has said in class, not all interpretations are equal; but experience and context affects the lens through which preachers are able to see the central issues in the text. I agree that to judge the validity of interpretations on the premise that each interpretation should be the same strictly using the details of the text is to attempt to put preachers in a straitjacket.[7] In order to reach the hearers, the preacher must be free to use his or her imagination and context in order to best serve the congregation.

Learning to find one's own voice as an African American preacher is without question one of the biggest hurdles to effective preaching.[8] This is because I have learned that people appreciate variety and expect individual authenticity. In my local church context people have come to expect and appreciate the varying styles of the associate ministers because the majority of us have found our own voice and do not persist in attempting to be carbon copies of our pastor. This is also why I believe that it is very important for preachers to learn from other preachers and pick up beneficial habits but also to resist the temptation to emulate others too much. This is the danger also of using commentaries because the preacher attempting to find his or her own voice can be completely drowned out by the interpretations of others. We as preachers should not be reliant on commentaries to feed our interpretations. The sermon building process should be a symphony of conversation partners and I agree that the preacher's voice should be fused with the other voices that contribute to a healthy interpretation of the text.⁹ Sermon development that produces a sermon that makes a difference cannot be performed in a vacuum but must allow the issues of the people to have a place at the table. Keeping this in mind will also help the preacher to keep his or her eye on the big picture of sermon development – that one of the goals of preach must be to help people and we cannot help them if we refuse to acknowledge the issues that they are dealing with.

On Christian Doctrine

The fourth book within *On Christian Doctrine* arrested my interest when it began covering the topic of eloquence in speaking and the rules of eloquence. It was interesting because Augustine helped me the see the already existent dialectic between communicating facts or truth and the eloquence with which these ideas are communicated. I could identify with the issue as a preacher of finding a balance between eloquence and freedom during the creative process so that ideas are not stifled by the stress due to the expectations of being eloquent. This is why for the majority of my preaching experience I have preached from a manuscript as I sought to be both eloquent and informative; to be careful about the words that I use while also conveying wisdom. This discussion led me to consider the temptations that preachers face to sacrifice wisdom or information in the name of eloquence and end up using terminology that is unfamiliar and in some cases confusing to the congregation such as the term pericope.

This dialectic informs my creative process when crafting sermons because I am initially more concerned about writing down what I believe God is conveying to me through the text as quickly as possible so as not to lose the information as I am concerned about my eloquence. This is because I believe that it is always possible to revisit and revise as long as there is information with which to start. I have found that I am intentional in my eloquence but not overly so because I do not want the text to be overshadowed by eloquence. Content or essential truth is the most important thing. I found the discussion surrounding the use of scripture as a substitute for eloquence helpful because it suggested that as preachers we may agree from time to time that scripture broaches a subject in a more eloquent way than we could.[10] Scripture has an advantage over the preacher in that scripture is something familiar and eloquent. A particular sentence that stayed with me as I continued to read included the words "For he who speaks eloquently is heard with pleasure; he who speaks wisely is heard with profit."[11] It reminded me that today some preachers preach for the pleasure of some persons' itching ears but not for the individual's profit. What we preach should be both eloquent and informative because either extreme would fall short.

---

[1] Harris, *Preaching Liberation*, 72.
[2] Ibid.
[3] Cf. Harris, *Preaching Liberation*, 73.
[4] Ibid., 34.
[5] Cf. Harris, *Preaching Liberation*, 34.
[6] Harris, *The Word Made Plain*, 53.
[7] Ibid.
[8] Ibid.
[9] Ibid.
[10] Cf. Saint Augustine, 122.
[11] Saint Augustine, 122.

Bibliography

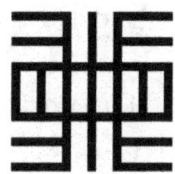

Bennis, Warren, and Burt Nanus. *Leaders: Strategies for Taking Charge*. New York, NY: HarperCollins Publishers, 2007.

Brand, Chad, Charles Draper, and Archie England. eds. *Holman Illustrated Bible Dictionary*. Nashville, TN: Holman Bible Publishers, 2003.

Brandon, S. G. F. *Jesus and the Zealots*. Manchester, UK: Manchester University Press, 1967.

Braxton, Brad. "Sanctification for Proclamation, Walking with God." Lecture, annual meeting of the Hampton University Ministers Conference, Hampton, VA, June 9, 2009.

Brown, Raymond E., Joseph A. Fitzmyer, and Roland E. Murphy. *The New Jerome Biblical Commentary*. Upper Saddle River, NJ: Prentice-Hall, Inc., 1990.

Carter, Jerry. "What Am I Preaching?" Lecture, annual meeting of the Hampton University Ministers Conference, Hampton, VA, June 8, 2010.

———. "Who Am I as Preacher?" Lecture, annual meeting of the Hampton University Ministers Conference, Hampton, VA, June 10, 2010.

Coogan, Michael D. Ed. *The New Oxford Annotated Bible with the Apocrypha. Augmented 3rd Edition*. New York, NY: Oxford University Press, 2007.

Dupont-Sommer, A. *The Jewish Sect of Qumrân and the Essenes: New Studies on the Dead Sea Scrolls.* Translated by R. D. Barnett. New York, NY: Macmillan, 1956.

Ehrman, Bart D. "The Gospel According to Paul: The Letter to the Romans." In *The New Testament: A Historical Introduction to the Early Christian Writings.* 4th ed. New York, NY: Oxford University Press, 2004.

———. *The New Testament: A Historical Introduction to the Early Christian Writings.* 4th. New York, NY: Oxford University Press, 2008.

Evans, James H., Jr. *We Have Been Believers: An African-American Systematic Theology.* Minneapolis, MN: Fortress Press, 1992.

Finkelstein, Israel, and Neil A. Silberman. *The Bible Unearthed: Archaeology's New Vision of Ancient Israel and the Origin of Its Sacred Texts.* New York, NY: The Free Press, 2001.

Finkelstein, Louis. "The Pharisees: Their Origin and Their Philosophy." *Harvard Theological Review* 22, no. 3 (1929): 185-261.

———. *The Pharisees: The Sociological Background of Their Faith.* Vol. I. Philadelphia, PA: Jewish Publication Society of America, 1938.

Forta, Arye. *Judaism.* Oxford, UK: Heinemann Educational, 1995.

Franklin, Robert M. *Crisis in the Village: Restoring Hope in African American Communities.* Minneapolis, MN: Fortress Press, 2007.

Friesen, Steven J. "Injustice or God's Will? Early Christian Explanations of Poverty." In *Wealth and Poverty in Early Church and Society*, edited by Susan R. Holman, 17-36. Grand Rapids, MI: Baker Academic, 2008.

Ginsburg, Christian D. *The Essenes: Their History and Doctrines and The Kabbalah: Its Doctrines, Development and Literature.* New York, NY: Cosimo, 2005.

González, Justo L. *Faith and Wealth: A History of Early Christian Ideas on the Origin, Significance, and Use of Money.* New York, NY: Harper and Row, 1990.

Bibliography

Goodman, Martin. "The Place of the Sadducees in First-Century Judaism." In *Redefining First-Century Jewish and Christian Identities: Essays in Honor of Ed Parish Sanders*, edited by Fabian E. Udoh, 139-152. Notre Dame, IN: University of Notre Dame Press, 2008.

Gorman, Michael J. *Elements of Biblical Exegesis*. Peabody, MA: Hendrickson, 2009.

Gowan, Donald E. "Wealth and Poverty in the Old Testament: The Case of the Widow, The Orphan, and the Sojourner." *Interpretation* 41, no. 4 (1987): 341-353.

Guthrie, Shirley C., Jr. *Christian Doctrine*. Louisville, KY: Westminster/John Knox Press, 1994.

Harrelson, Walter J. ed. *The New Interpreter's Study Bible*. Nashville, TN: Abingdon Press, 2003.

Harris, James H. *Preaching Liberation*. Minneapolis, MN: Fortress Press, 1995.

———. *The Word Made Plain: The Power and Promise of Preaching*. Minneapolis, MN: Fortress Press, 2004.

Hatina, Thomas R. "Jewish Religious Backgrounds of the New Testament: Pharisees and Sadducees as Case Studies." In *Approaches to New Testament Study*, edited by Stanley E. Porter, and David Tombs, 46-76. Sheffield, UK: Sheffield Academic Press Ltd, 1995.

Haynes, Frederick D., III. *Healing Our Broken Village*. Dallas, TX: Saint Paul Press, 2008.

Hengel, Martin. *The Zealots: Investigations into the Jewish Freedom Movement in the Period from Herod I Until 70 A.D.* Translated by David Smith. Edinburgh, UK: T. and T. Clark, 1989.

Hicks, H. Beecher, Jr. *Preaching Through A Storm*. Grand Rapids, MI: Zondervan, 1987.

Hopkins, Dwight N. *Down, Up and Over: Slave Religion and Black Theology*. Minneapolis, MN: Fortress Press, 2000.

Horsley, Richard A. "The Zealots: their origin, relationships and importance in the Jewish Revolt." *Novum Testamentum* 28, no. 2 (1986): 159-192.

Humphreys, Fisher, and Philip Wise. *Fundamentalism.* Macon, GA: Smyth and Helwys Publishing, 2004.

Knitter, Paul F. *No Other Name?: A Critical Survey of Christian Attitudes Toward the World Religions.* 1985. Reprint. Maryknoll, NY: Orbis Books, 1999.

LaRue, Cleophus J. "How Do I Get Better at the Foolishness of Preaching Part II." Lecture, annual meeting of the Hampton University Ministers Conference, Hampton, VA, June 7, 2007.

———. ed. *Power in the Pulpit: How America's Most Effective Black Preachers Prepare Their Sermons.* Louisville, KY: Westminster John Knox Press, 2002.

———. *I Believe I'll Testify: The Art of African American Preaching.* Louisville, KY: Westminster John Knox Press, 2011.

———. *The Heart of Black Preaching.* Louisville, KY: Westminster John Knox Press, 2000.

Levine, Amy-Jill. "Luke's Pharisees." In *In Quest of the Historical Pharisees*, edited by Jacob Neusner, and Bruce D. Chilton, 113-130. Waco, TX: Baylor University Press, 2007.

Lindsay, D. Michael. "Connected Churches Support Spiritual Transformation." In *Friendship: Creating a Culture of Connectivity in Your Church*, edited by Dave Thornton. Loveland, CO: Group Publishing, 2005.

Loader, William R. G. *Journal for the Study of the New Testament, no 63,* 1996, p 45-61

Macquarrie, John. *Jesus Christ in Modern Thought.* 1990. Reprint. Harrisburg, PA: Trinity Press International, 1991.

McDonough, Reginald M. *Keys to Effective Motivation: Constructive Ideas for Helping Members to Get Involved in the Life and Work of the Church.* Nashville, TN: Broadman Press, 1979.

McGrath, Alister E. *Christian Theology: An Introduction.* 5th. West Sussex, UK: Wiley-Blackwell, 2011.

Migliore, Daniel L. *Faith Seeking Understanding: An Introduction to Christian Theology.* 2nd. Grand Rapids, MI: Wm. B. Eerdmans Publishing Co., 2004.

Miller, Madeleine S., and J. Lane Miller. *Harper's Encyclopedia of Bible Life.* 3rd Revised. New York, NY: Harper and Row, 1978.

Mills, Watson E. ed. *Mercer Dictionary of the Bible.* Macon, GA: Mercer University Press, 1991.

Murphy, Catherine M. *Wealth in the Dead Sea Scrolls and in the Qumran Community.* Leiden, NL: Brill, 2001.

Murrow, David. "Leadership and the Masculine Spirit." In *Why Men Hate Going to Church.* Nashville, TN: Thomas Nelson Inc., 2005.

Musser, Donald W., and Joseph L. Price. *New and Enlarged Handbook of Christian Theology.* Nashville, TN: Abingdon Press, 2003.

Niebuhr, H. Richard. *Christ and Culture.* 1951. Reprint. New York, NY: HarperOne, 2001.

———. *The Purpose of the Church and Its Ministry.* 1956. Reprint. New York, NY: Harper and Row, 1977.

Phillips, Thomas E. "Revisiting Philo: Discussions of Wealth and Poverty in Philo's Ethical Discourse." *Journal for The Study of The New Testament,* no. 83 (2001): 111-121.

Phipps, William E. "Jesus, the Prophetic Pharisee." *Journal of Ecumenical Studies* 41, no. 1 (1977): 17-31.

Pilgrim, Walter E. *Good News to the Poor.* Minneapolis, MN: Augsburg Publishing House, 1981.

Poole, Matthew. *A Commentary on the Holy Bible.* Vols. Volume II: Psalms-Malachi. III vols. Peabody, MA: Hendrickson, 1985.

Proctor, Samuel D. *The Certain Sound of the Trumpet: Crafting a Sermon of Authority.* Valley Forge, PA: Judson Press, 1994.

Rauschenbusch, Walter. *Christianity and the Social Crisis.* Louisville, KY: Westminster/John Knox Press, 1991.

Reinhartz, Adele. "Crucifying Caiaphas: Hellenism and the High Priesthood in Life of Jesus Narratives." In *Redefining First-Century Jewish and Christian Identities: Essays in Honor of Ed Parish*

Sanders, edited by Fabian E. Udoh, 227-245. Notre Dame, IN: University of Notre Dame Press, 2008.

Saint Augustine. *On Christian Doctrine.* Translated by D. W. Robertson, Jr. Upper Saddle River, NJ: Prentice Hall, 1958.

Saldarini, Anthony J. *Pharisees, Scribes and Pharisees in Palestinian Society.* Grand Rapids, MI: Wm. B. Eerdmans, 2001.

Sanders, Cheryl J. *Empowerment Ethics for a Liberated People: A Path to African American Social Transformation.* Minneapolis, MN: Fortress Press, 1995.

———. "Preaching for Advocacy through Love." Lecture, annual meeting of the Hampton University Ministers Conference, Hampton, VA, June 6, 2007.

Sanders, J. Oswald. *Spiritual Leadership: Principles of Excellence for Every Believer.* Chicago, IL: Moody Press, 2007.

Shawchuck, Norman, and Roger Heuser. *Leading the Congregation: Caring for Yourself While Serving the People.* Nashville, TN: Abingdon Press, 1993.

Simmons, William A. *Peoples of the New Testament World: An Illustrated Guide.* Peabody, MA: Hendrickson, 2008.

Smith, Christian. *The Emergence of Liberation Theology: Radical Religion and Social Movement Theory.* Chicago, IL: University of Chicago Press, 1991.

Smith, David L. *A Handbook of Contemporary Theology: Tracing Trends and Discerning Directions in Today's Theological Landscape.* Grand Rapids, MI: BridgePoint Books, 1998.

Soulen, Richard N., and R. Kendall Soulen. *Handbook of Biblical Criticism.* 3rd Edition Revised and Expanded. Louisville, KY: Westminster John Knox Press, 2001.

Sutphin, Stanley T. *Options in Contemporary Theology.* Washington, DC: University Press of America, 1977.

Thomas, Frank A. *They Like to Never Quit Praisin' God: The Role of Celebration in Preaching.* Cleveland, OH: The Pilgrim Press, 1997.

Thurman, Howard. *Jesus and the Disinherited.* Boston, MA: Beacon Press, 1996.

Tidwell, Charles A. *Church Administration: Effective Leadership for Ministry*. Nashville, TN: Broadman Press, 1985.

Warren, Rick. "Organizing Around Your Purposes." In *The Purpose-Driven Church*. Grand Rapids, MI: Zondervan, 1995.

Weaver, J. Denny. *The Nonviolent Atonement*. 2nd. Grand Rapids, MI: Wm. B. Eerdmans Publishing Co., 2011.

Wenell, Karen. *Expository Times* 117, no. 4 (Jan. 2006): 153-154.

Williams, Pat. *The Leadership Wisdom of Solomon*. Cincinnati, OH: Standard Publishing, 2010.

www.ingramcontent.com/pod-product-compliance
Lightning Source LLC
Chambersburg PA
CBHW050633300426
44112CB00012B/1779